MW01292072

A Reasonable Faith

CAN YOU BE SMART AND BELIEVE IN
THE BIBLE, GOD, AND FAITH?

RUBENS RUBA

WESTBOW
P R E S S
A DIVISION OF THOMAS NELSON

WestBow Press books may be ordered through booksellers or by contacting:

WestBow Press
A Division of Thomas Nelson
1663 Liberty Drive
Bloomington, IN 47403
www.westbowpress.com
1-(866) 928-1240

Because of the dynamic nature of the Internet, any web addresses or links contained in this book may have changed since publication and may no longer be valid. The views expressed in this work are solely those of the author and do not necessarily reflect the views of the publisher, and the publisher hereby disclaims any responsibility for them.

Any people depicted in stock imagery provided by Thinkstock are models, and such images are being used for illustrative purposes only.

Certain stock imagery © Thinkstock.

ISBN: 978-1-4497-1406-2 (sc)
ISBN: 978-1-4497-1407-9 (e)

Library of Congress Control Number: 2011924439

Printed in the United States of America

WestBow Press rev. date: 03/14/2011

To Jeff & LeAnn,
May God continue to make you "bold" in your wittness!!

With love, prayers and much appreciation,

This book is dedicated to:

My supportive wife – Beth who has been my greatest source of encouragement

My wonderful daughters whom I am proud of – Abigail and Elizabeth

My Mother and Father in Law – John and Carol Mangle

A Loving Church - Lewisburg Alliance Church, Lewisburg, Pennsylvania

2011

Contents

Can you be smart and be a person of faith?

In May of 2010, the commencement speaker at Bucknell University, Lewisburg, Pennsylvania was a distinguished, physician, Dr. Ben Carson of Johns Hopkins Medical Center. He is renowned in the field of *Pediatric Neurosurgery*. He has over 40 honorary doctorate degrees. He is also a member of the American Academy of Achievement, the Horatio Alger Association of Distinguished Americans, and the Alpha Omega Honor Medical Society. He is the President and co-founder of the Carson Scholars Fund, which recognizes young people of all backgrounds for exceptional academic and humanitarian accomplishments. Further, on June 19, 2008, Dr. Carson received the Presidential Medal of Freedom from President George W. Bush.

His original claim to fame occurred In September 1987, when Dr. Carson performed a procedure to separate a pair of seven-month-old German conjoined twins, who were joined at the head. Carson was the lead surgeon on the team which performed the complex procedure. Then, in 1997, Carson and his team went to South Africa to separate Joseph and Luka Banda, infant boys from Zambia. Both boys survived, and neither one suffered severe brain damage. The Bandas were the first set of twins joined at the tops of their heads to be successfully surgically separated. [1] Yet, as he was announced to speak at the Bucknell University Commencement 2010, a small number, yet vocal group of professors and students made an appeal to the administration that he would be "uninvited" because he is "unscientific, since he believes in the Biblical account of Creation, faith, and the Bible."

As an evangelical Christian, and the Senior Pastor *of Lewisburg Alliance Church*, in Lewisburg, Pennsylvania I was greatly interested in the discussion on two levels. First, I was amazed that in the college world, where there is such pride in 'free' and 'open' thinking, that Christianity, faith and the Bible, would be regarded as lacking credibility, by some in the university world. But second, I am concerned that the students at Bucknell University, as well as the entire community of Lewisburg would be left without a "balanced" response in <u>favor</u> of Christianity. It is my hope that each reader would be truly open-minded, and that you will find that having a Christian world view is reasonable and rationale.

For those readers who would categorize themselves as having been "born again" – the type that results in a conversion, my prayer is that you will come away with a new found boldness in your faith. For those who are *<u>annoyed</u>* by the first group of *<u>born again</u>* Christians my prayer is that as you continue to read this book, you may understand the first group better, and as a result, maybe they will *not* annoy you as much. To the third group of readers who have made up

---

1   Biographical Information of Dr. B. A. Carson obtained through Wikipedia.org

their mind <u>already</u> that Christianity is unreasonable and irrational, I hope that you do read it, and overcome your biases and fears, and actually understand, not a stereotype of Christianity, but the rationale reasoning behind the dogmatic posturing.

Bucknell University is a great school of higher learning. I have many friends who teach, administrate, and attend as students. I do believe that the school and it's administration has done a good job in attempting to provide a dialogue for the school. But this is issue is not just about Bucknell. From my perspective it is about the place that Christ and Christianity plays in our society. Bucknell University's experience with Dr. Carson's religious beliefs should serve as a forum for all of us to have deeper discussions.

In many ways, you will find this book to be a book about theology. Theology, in its simplest level, is but *the explanation of what Christians believe about God*. I am a Pastor, and my background is theological. Yet the problem, as I see with many 'theological books" is that most of them, are written by well meaning authors who try to string words together like…*"The Biblical relativism in our society fails to correspond to the pragmatism and realism."* Somehow, reading some of those books adds confusion and do not clearly speak to the issues at hand.

So, without trying to oversimplify the subject, I want to do my level best to help you understand the Bible, Christ, and His Church, and to provide a platform of discussion of why the Christian Faith is reasonable.

Is this book really needed?

The conflict with Christianity is not just seen in the University level. At the writing of this book, Oprah has announced that this is her last year for her afternoon television show. And for some reason, I just don't believe that Oprah is going to retire completely. But, as a result of her television show there has been a strong acceptance of a philosophy of life which "blends" a variety of spiritual faiths, and deems them all acceptable. From New Age Meditation, to Christian Orthodoxy, Oprah persuades her listeners that all religious beliefs are acceptable, and that there are many ways to feel that 'inner peace.' Philosophers have dubbed our era as a postmodern one which relativism reigns supreme. Oops! I promised not to use those types of phrases, didn't I? So, here is a better one: Oprah's philosophy is: *Whatever works for you, do it!*

I believe that this philosophy of life is in direct opposition to Biblical and Historical teaching. For Christianity is designed to be an *exclusive* faith. It has always been puzzling to hear that a number of Roman Catholics and Evangelical proclaim themselves to be Christians, yet "dabble" in all sorts of Far East practices. This dual commitment is in direct contradiction to the Bible's account, as well as historical Christian teaching. When someone mentions the exclusiveness of Christ, the reaction of people is usually filled with opposition and anger. How dare Christians claim that Christ is the only path to God? That is arrogant and egotistical.

But the problem goes deeper than the struggle with a Universalist approach to religion. For even those who are "church going" and "card carrying" Christians are swaying to the pressure to be all-inclusive. Check out these statistics which on the surface can be rather encouraging to Christianity, yet cause us in church leadership to cringe![2]

- 80 percent of all Americans describe themselves as "spiritual."

- 80 percent believe that God created the Universe.

- 66 percent say they pray every day.

- 85 percent consider themselves Christian.

All that sounds rather encouraging until you begin to look under the surface and you discover that there has been erosion. For though those statistics look great, consider the following:

- Only 45 percent of those who profess to be Christian attend worship services weekly.

- Almost 70 percent of self proclaimed Evangelical Christians believe that there is more than one way to heaven.

---

2   Josh McDowell and Bob Hostetler, <u>The New Tolerance</u>, (Wheaton, Il., Tyndale Publishers, 1988 p. 174).

- Almost 70 percent of incoming freshman at Christian colleges say there are no moral absolutes.

- And 84 percent of those collegians are unable to explain basic Christian beliefs.

Something is wrong. Clearly there is a clear disconnect from Biblical Truth. In Oprah's world, there is a smorgasbord of beliefs and spiritual ideas that everyone can pick or choose.

My contention is that Christianity cannot be placed in the mix of choices among many religions. Christianity, by its very nature, is head and shoulders above every other religion. For instance, The Bible is not just one word of God, among many, but it is solely the Word of God. And Jesus did not proclaim to be one of the ways to God. He states clearly that *"He is the way, the truth and the life"* (John 14:6). Jesus himself proclaims to be the only way!

R.C. Sproul was once asked, *"What is the difference between the Christian God and the gods of other religions?"* In a simple way, he gave the answer. He said, *"The God of Christianity exists."* [3] As some of you read R.C. Sproul's statement, you immediately began to think how that sounds very arrogant! How dare you put Christianity above Judaism, Islam or any other religion?

My contention in this book is that this is not arrogance, but it is the "historical and Biblical position" of Christianity. For in university campuses all over our nation, as well as in the general population of our country, there has been such a sensitivity to conform and sacrifice truth in the altar of peace and for the sake of fairness and unity.

---

3   R.C. Sproul, Reasons to Believe. Zondervan Publications: Grand Rapids, Michigan, p.116.

Through this book, I want to answer some basic questions that distinguish Christ from the other gods of this world. My desire is not to offend, but to present the reasons why I believe in God, the Bible, and Christ, who is the only hope for eternal life. It is to bring a reasonable and rational understanding, and thereby encourage Christians to defend their faith. It is to present to skeptics that Christianity is not just for weak minded people, who have no rationale for their faith. It is to bring to the students on college campuses, as well as church going people that there is a *"reasonable"* argument for God, the Bible and faith. In other words, you do not have to check out your brains in order to believe in Christianity. It is reasonable and rationale!

CHAPTER ONE

Does Science "trump" Faith?

My father was born in the Ukraine, and came to United States by way of Brasil in the mid 1960's. He was a great man of faith, and strongly believed in the Bible as God's supreme Word to man. Yet, since his childhood, progress has been made in the fields of math, science, not to mention transportation, as well as communication. Then, there are the remarkable advances in medicine, technology, as well as sub-atomic physics. All these advances give each of us a feeling of confidence to the point that the very idea of God seems strangely dated. No wonder Christians are looked upon as old fashioned with their preaching of God and Satan. Christians seem to be stuck in a time warp, representative of the new "Brady Bunch" movies, where Mike and Carol Brady were stuck in their 1970's clothes.

Recently, I spoke to a college student who told me that the reason why they do not attend church was because they were convinced that *Religion* was needed for his parents, but he didn't really need God in his life right now. When

I pressed him on why he felt that way, he mentioned that "society has progressed, and we know a lot more about earth and space than his parents ever did. I must admit that much of the television reporting seems to substantiate or confirm his suspicions. As a result, there seems to be a deep valley that is unable to be crossed between science and faith.

A great proponent of this view is a man by the name of Richard Dawkins who was a Zoologist. He stated:

> *What has theology ever said that is of the smallest use to anybody? What has theology ever said that is demonstrably true and is not obvious?*[4]

The man on the street may not be as "in your face" as Richard Dawkins, but that attitude exists where ditching the idea of God or faith has become popular in our society. Yet, it was not always that way!

Was Science always against Christianity?

As you look at the key players of the "early science" movement, there seems to have been a marriage of the two that is understated in our society's discussions. For instance, Richard Dawkins belief was completely out of sync with the scientific minds of the 16th Century. For during that period of time, modern science grew at a tremendous pace. That growth came as a result of the enlightenment period. What's more, it was initiated by Christians. Let me name of few:

1. *Francis Bacon* was an English philosopher, statesman, lawyer and scientist who lived in the early 1600's. He is known as the Father of "empiricism." Empiricism is a theory that asserts that all knowledge arises from *evidence*

---

4   Richard Dawkins.net/*Emptiness of Theology*, from Free Inquiry Magazine, Vol. 18,, Number 2, 2006.

gathered through *experience*. Yet, this was not a negative perspective against Christianity. He saw both God's creation and the Bible as critical to his ability to interpret the world.[5]

2. *Johannes Kepler* was a German Mathematician who became a renowned astronomer and astrologer in the 17th century. He discovered that earth traveled around the sun. He perceived himself to follow after God in his research. He viewed himself as a partner with God when he stated, that he was *"thinking God's thoughts after him."*[6]

3. *Galileo and Copernicus* are names that are universally recognizable. Both Christian men were convinced that their work glorified God. And this, in spite of living in a time where the religious authorities rejected the spread of knowledge.

4. *Sir Isaac Newton was a physicist and mathematician who* wrote his *Principia* in the assurance that *"this world could originate from nothing, but the perfectly free will of God."*[7] There was a rumor that he spent more time in the Bible than in scientific research.

5. *Max Planck* is probably a name you do not recognize unless you are/were a physics major. He lived from 1858-1947 and he is best known

5 Freebase.com/*Empircism*
6 Job Kozhamthadam, *The discovery of Kepler's Laws: The Interaction between science, Philosophy and Religion*, University of Notre Dame Press, 1993.
7 Sir Isaac Newton, *The Principia: Mathematical Principles of Natural Philosophy*. University of California, 1999.

for his work in *Quantum Theory*, which assisted great in understanding atomic and sub-atomic worlds. His writings are well document that he believe in a sovereign and creative God. In 1918, he won the Nobel Peace Prize for his work.[8]

6. *Michael Faraday* (of the 19th Century) was known for his work in electricity. He was a devout Presbyterian who wanted to break away from the State Church, and wanted to bring the church back to the New Testament roots. His view of nature was greatly influenced by Christianity.

7. Albert Einstein is a name that everyone would recognize. He was known for the famous conversion of matter into energy ($E=mc2$). Many people do not realize that, though he was not a committed Christian, nonetheless, he ruled out a universe that was non-created. He firmly denied "atheism." He said on one occasion: *"I have repeatedly said that in my opinion the idea of a personal God is a childlike one. You may call me an agnostic, but I do not share the crusading spirit of the professional atheist whose fervor is mostly due to a painful act of liberation from the fetters of religious indoctrination received in youth. I prefer an attitude of humility corresponding to the weakness of our intellectual understanding of nature and of our own being."[9]* This and many other pioneers bring to light that science and

---

8 Nobelprize.org/Max Planck.
9 Albert Einstein to Guy H. Raner Jr., Sept. 28, 1949, quoted by Michael R. Gilmore in Skeptic magazine, Vol. 5, No. 2

religion need not be in opposition, and early on in history it was not.

Caution: Early Scientists were not Believers

Yet, it would be erroneous, to think that scientists were "*committed and strong believers*" in those early days, while making today's scientists to be agnostics or even atheists. That comparison is not based in reality. Though they believed in God and maybe even the Church, a personal relationship would be far from an accurate description of their commitment.

A research study was taken by *Elaine Ecklund*, and Christopher Scheitle in *2007 which was very interesting*. They questioned 2,198 faculty members in the disciplines of physics, chemistry, biology, sociology, economics, political science, and psychology from 21 elite U.S. research universities.[10] Overall, 75% of professors contacted actually completed the survey. Among the different disciplines, disbelief in the existence of God was not correlated with any particular area of expertise:

- In the fields of Physics, Chemistry and Biology the average percentage of those who did NOT believe in God was 37.6%.

- At the same time, they found that approximately 40% were believers in God.

- Yet, 20% did not commit either way.

There have always that this number has been very consistent through the century.

---

10 *Ecklund, E. H. and C. P. Scheitle. Religion among Academic Scientists: Distinctions, Disciplines, and Demographics. Social Problems 54: 289–307.*

The point being, that there have <u>always</u> been atheists and Christians who are scientists, as in other fields of study. Historically, there were many from the Enlightenment period that had a disregard for God.

Why is there opposition between Science and God?

But why? Why is there such contempt for God, in the scientific world? To answer this question, we need to review three people who were the most prominent voices for the atheistic movement. Their understanding and use of science have changed the world's attitudes towards God.

The three men are *Sigmund Freud, Karl Marx, and Charles Darwin.* During their popularity, religion came to be seen in educational circles as emotional, or illusionary. It was in many ways seen as a society necessity until science could catch up.

1. *<u>Sigmund Freud</u>* was Jewish but grew up in highly Roman Catholic neighborhood. He admits that as a Jewish person he experienced a great amount of anti-Semitic hatred. As a result, his view of religion was one which he saw as negative. He worked for many years in attempting to undermine religion. He desired to replace religious theology which saw people as sinners who needed God as a solution to their problems. He further believed that men created a god in their own image. The interesting side note is that his theories are ***not*** and ***never were*** science of any real kind. His views were really a type of personal acceptance of his own incapacities. As John F. Kihlstrom writes, *"While Freud had an enormous impact on 20th century culture, his influence on psychology has been that of a dead weight. At best, Freud is a figure of only a historical interest for psychologists. He is better studied as a writer, in departments of language and literature,*

than as a scientist, Psychologists can get along without him."[11]Is *Freud Still Alive? No, Not Really*, by John F. Kihlstro)

2. *Karl Marx* believed that the world consists only of matter without any spiritual dimensions. He believed that every aspect of life is determined by social and political factors. The very idea of God is merely a human attempt to deal with the harshness of life that a person would have experienced. In fact, he went as far as saying "*The abolition of religion as the illusory happiness of the people is required for real happiness. The demand to give up the illusions about its condition is the demand to give up a condition that needs illusions.*[12] In other words, for you to truly be happy, you need to rid yourself of all religion. He then believed that social revolution would be the great liberator of humanity. As communism would gain strength, religion would decline.

That was his view, though it did not succeed. Whenever socialism has been introduced there has been bloodshed. Communism has failed whether one looks into Russia in 1917 to the many of the Eastern European nations of the 20th century. In fact, the people who stood out against it at enormous cost were the Christians Books have been written of the persecution, such as coming from well known author *Alexander Solzhenitsyn*. It is safe to say that Marxism does not work. Atheism failed in Russia, as well as Eastern Europe. It is also failing in Cuba and China, the only places in the world that is still attempting to make it work. The jury is still out on those two countries.

---

11 John F. Kihlstrom, *Is Freud Still Alive? No, Not Really. Hilgard's Introduction to Psychology*, 13th Ed, New York: Harcourt Brace Jovanovich, 2000.
12 Marxism On Religion, D. McLellan, The Macmillan Press Ltd 1987, p. 42.

3. The third influential person was *Charles Darwin*. Interestingly, he was considering ordination as a young man, but his interest in the sciences were too much of a temptation. I find it puzzling that in some academic schools, it is rather fashionable to think of Darwin as the darling of the atheists. Yet, this would be rather foolish. For if you really took time to read Darwin's views about God, it would be confusing and would not maintain rational reasoning.

As he grew older his unbelief in God became stronger. In fact, allow me to give you two main reasons for this movement in his life. First, came as a result of the death of his daughter. And second, the church's doctrine of hell, which was very popular during the Victorian age of preachers caused him to enter into a deeper disbelief of God. These two issues became areas of struggle for Darwin. The point here is that these two areas were what caused his movement away from God, and not his theory of natural selection.

Evolution cannot be an arbiter of truth!

I want to be abundantly clear that the theory of evolution is a theory. It sets out to explain that various forms of life have developed from more simple forms over millions of years. A belief in a Creator sets out to explain that there is a great mind behind all matter. My point is that there is contradiction between the two.

The best statement that I can possibly give is from *Stephen Jay Gould,* who was one of the world's greatest proponents on the theory of evolution. He is correct when he says:

> *"To say for the umpteenth (time)...science simply cannot adjudicate the issue of God's possible superintendence of nature. We neither affirm or deny it. We simply cannot comment on it as scientists. If some of our crowd have made untoward statements claiming that Darwinism*

disapproves God then I will find Mrs. McInerney (his old schoolmistress!) and have their knuckles rapped for it…"[13]

The key word he used is "adjudicate." Adjudicate means, "to settle a case." In other words, there isn't anything in the scientific method that can either prove God's existence or disprove it. Yet, the evidence pointing to an intelligent design can be reasonably attained. Yet, I would warn the reader not to place your entire future based only on the "evidence" or "lack of evidence in science. There is so much more that should be considered than an analysis of physics or chemical constituents. For these cannot explain human behavior, morals, speech and even worship. In the next few chapters, we want to consider the evidence for God, the reliability of the Bible, and the sole claim by Christ to be the only "Savior" of the world. Keep an open mind and be open to truth.

---

13 *Stephen Gould, Rock of Ages: Science and Religion in the fullness of life, Ballantine, 1999.)*

CHAPTER TWO:

Is there evidence of God?

If science and religion are not competitors in the search for truth, then is there any evidence _for_ God?

The other day, I was at a local store in our town, and as I was waiting my turn to pay the cashier, two ladies were discussing a FOX News report that they had seen the prior evening. They had both watched the show where there was a panel debating whether the President of the United States was a Christian or a Muslim. After going back and forth, one of the ladies finally said..."_I don't see what the big deal is anyway, I personally do not believe there is a God, it really doesn't matter_! Now, that position is understandable in a way. But unless you think that the reason why many people deny God is mostly "intellectually based," let me give you a thought. My contention is that there are a number of reasons why people reject the existence of God and many of them are not as a result of intellectual problems with Christianity but issues of the heart and experience.

For instance, they reject the existence of God, because they have lost someone or something that they loved very much. Like Darwin. In the midst of a painful experience, at the loss of his sister, it is inconceivable to think of a sovereign God who would allow such a thing to happen. Their experiences demand that they deny the existence of a personal God.

But I do admit that there are those who are very analytical and they struggle with "faith over reason." Therefore, let me attempt to give us a step toward by providing a framework on the question of the existence of God.

Why can't God be studied in a Test Tube?

First, examining God can be quite a challenge since He would never fit into a test tube in a lab. When I was in High School in Philadelphia, my science teacher drilled into me that in order for something to be scientifically proved, it must be repeatable. A scientist does not announce a new finding to the world on the basis of one experiment or even a theory. That is why the process of getting a new pharmaceutical drug onto the market takes such a long time. The problem with approaching "the evidence of God" or even the "validity of the Bible" is that they require a certain amount of faith in historical facts.[14] And since the Scientific method requires repetition, and history cannot be repeated or replicated, we are then, at a stalemate. The other night I was watching the movie "*Back to the Future*" with Michael J. Fox, and I was thinking how great it would be to go back in time and replay or even change an event. Only in Hollywood can you do that! In real life you can't go back and redo the creation, or even the crucifixion of Christ. Yet,

---

14 Michael Green, Avoiding Jesus.Baker Books: Grand Rapids, Michigan, p. 44-45.

even if those events could not be proven through repetition, it does not necessarily mean that those events didn't occur. Therefore, the evidence of God has to be verified through a number of other methods. What other ways can we discuss that would bring light to the question of the evidence for God that goes beyond the review of science? There are three issues that come to mind.

1. The Problem of Suffering

When my wife Beth and I were married, I was a youth pastor at First Baptist Church in Danville, Pennsylvania. It is a great church with some wonderful people who really try to live out their faith. It was over a year into our marriage that we found out that we were going to be expecting a baby. Other couples in our church were also expecting, and the excitement grew each month as we were closer to the due date. About the 6th month, we found out that there were some problems with the formation of our child. Through various tests they determined that our baby was hydrocephalic (fluid around the brain) and had Spina Bifida (which is a birth defect affecting the backbone and spinal canal). This was a real blow to our faith. For the next 3 months, we prayed, fasted and asked God to somehow perform a miracle, and heal our little child. But, as we chose to take our baby to term, God saw fit to take our child to be with him in heaven. I was a Pastor but in the months after our "little Bethany's" death, we were both hurting deeply. Beth and I went into a depression, and it was one of the hardest moments in our lives when we buried her. After the funeral and for the next few months I must admit that my faith was fainting. I felt very lost and wondered if I could really trust in the Lord ever again. My emotions went from anger, frustration, depression mingled by a few moments of faith. It was a roller coaster ride as both of us tried to work through the pain and hurt and I wondered if I could ever really trust in God ever again? I wondered if God was worthy of being trusted? But in the midst of the pain, we begin to lean on what "up to this moment" was purely an intellectual knowledge of God based on years of academic education. I began each day to see how God was able to turn our lives around, and renew our faith in him. And this is probably a subject for another book, but it is my way of saying that suffering can drive even those of us who are in ministry, and have committed our lives to Christ to the brink of faithless humility. But if you hang in there and you really trust in God he will renew your faith and your joy. How do I know that? Because I've experience it. I've seen God turn my sadness into Joy. I've seen God answer our prayers with two wonderful daughters, and one in heaven.

It was Pascal who in the midst of considering God stated that man was a great mystery. On the one hand, *he is a creature of the greatest grandeur, while on the other hand he is the worst misery.* That is probably an accurate account. For people who go through suffering, have found that their pain is one of the great obstacles for not believing in God.

And some struggle not only with their own personal painful experiences, but they notice the pain of others, which greatly affects them. They look at those who live in remote and poverty filled places all around the world, and wonder, "Where is this good God in the midst of all this pain?" Or they view a family member suffering through cancer and think, "How could God allow so much suffering in a life?" Please understand, I do not want to minimize any of the pain that we see, for one moment. It is by far the greatest argument against the existence of God. It is greater than any philosophical, theological or scientific argument.

But the alternative answers to painful experiences are even more confusing.

1. An <u>Atheist</u> would merely say, "There is no god. Do the best you can with the cards you've been dealt."

2. In <u>Dualism/Mysticism</u> good and evil are two sides of the same coin. It states that because there is two opposing sides to everything (ying and yang), you cannot experience true joy unless there is pain. Pain cannot be understood without joy. And joy cannot be understood without pain. Though this can make sense, it still does not provide a proper understanding of how to deal with pain. Explanations just go so far to comfort.

3. Many of the Eastern religions believe in what is called <u>illusionism</u>. Illusionism states that what I may think to be evil is actually good. Evil is only an illusion. In other words, maybe the pain or death is not a bad thing – think positively of the situation. Try to share that encouraging thought to a person who has just lost a child and see how far that gets you?

4. The <u>frustrated-god</u> states that maybe God would love to get rid of the pain in the world, but somehow isn't able. He has limits. He is good, but he just is not sovereign. All those alternative answers cannot truly answer the following questions. Who originated evil? What can be done about evil? Is there a way out of evil? And will evil always be a problem for me? The first four alternatives merely mask the pain. They merely try to help us deal with

the reality of a painful experience, but it never seems to completely go away.

5. The only alternative is the Christian _Monotheistic Trinitarian_ view. This view states that the God who exists is a good God. Though evil is in the world, someday the universe will be rid of any type of painful suffering. For in God's Son, Jesus Christ, He has paid, by dying on the cross for our sins, the penalty of sin and death. And those who place their hope in Christ will experience eternal life in a perfect environment called Heaven. But those who reject Christ's sacrifice, they will experience eternal punishment in Hell.

My basic point is that the Christian view of suffering and pain has a greater insight into the difficult problem of suffering than any of the other philosophies of life that you adopt.

For the Scriptures teach us that God is no stranger to pain. He did not just create the world, and then leave it at its most critical time. He does not willingly take joy in punishing us. It is the very opposite. He cares so much about the pain of this world that He became personally involved. He came as a man among men. He lived in poverty and suffering. He knew thirst and hunger. He experienced flogging and disappointment. His life even ended in one of the most painful ways known to mankind. He died on a cross.

For just a moment, allow me to encourage you the reader, to take a long look at the cross. For through the cross of Christ, God is telling you that **_God does care about your pain._** He cares so much that he came to share our struggle.

The cross tells us that God loves us even in the midst of pain and suffering.

Moreover, through that cross I see yet another truth: that somehow *God uses the pain in my life*. He turns evil into good. For it was evil, real evil, that crucified Jesus. And yet, He overcame evil. He turned hatred to love towards His persecutors. He gave an example of innocent and uncomplaining suffering that have inspired people ever since.

In researching this book, I found an interesting story of a man by the name of *Bishop John Leonard Wilson*.[15] *Bishop Wilson* gives God the credit for his own ability to forgive his captors and win the hearts of the Japanese Prison camp after the Second World War. On December 8, 1941, the Japanese invaded Malaya and advanced rapidly down the Peninsula. Two months later Singapore was compelled to surrender. Among those who were interned in the famous *Changi Jail* was the Bishop of Singapore, Bishop Leonard Wilson. The conditions in the prison were indescribable. The cells were crowded so that the prisoners couldn't even lie down. They were forbidden to talk. They had no water except for a toilet, and the prisoners were kept like this for eight months. The daily tortures caused the death of many of those prisoners. Yet, Bishop Wilson turned to his understanding of the cross of Christ to express forgiveness to his own torturers. The Bishop relates in his biography the following account:

> *"After my first beating, I was almost afraid to pray for courage, lest I should have another opportunity for exercising it. And when I muttered "Forgive them, I wondered how far I was being dramatic.*

15 a Transcribed sermon from Saint John's Review 15 (January, 1948): p 15-20 as well as a book by John Hayter, *Priest in Prison: Four years of Life in Japanese-occupied Singapore 1991*, Tynron Press.

> *And if I really meant it. I looked at their faces as they stood around taking turns to flog me. Their expressions were hard and cruel. And some of them were enjoying their cruelty."[16]*

Two years after the war was over and he had been released, he returned to Singapore and met one of his torturers face to face. That "torturer" stated:

> *'Each time I tortured you, you prayed that I might be forgiven. At first, this made me angry. But then it made me curious. Eventually your prayer brought me to Christ.[17]*

The point is that the cross is God's testimony that **He does care**, and that **God uses the pain** to actually strengthen us and refine our lives. But God's willingness to be involved in our situation is not just by way of example. For the life and death of Christ tells us something else of God. It also tells us that **God was victorious of sin and death.** On Good Friday, Jesus died with victory on his lips. He triumphed over pain, hatred, suffering and death. He rose from the dead and walked out of that tomb on the third day. From that day on he enjoys the power of an endless life. And he promises the same to those who are His followers. Christians who put their faith on Him understand the power of the Resurrection and how important it was that Jesus did rise again. For Jesus himself said, in 1 Corinthians 15, "*Because I live, you too shall live.*" For through the resurrection, it proved that God was not a victim of the cruelty of men in

---

16 John Hayter, *Priest in Prison: Four years of Life in Japanese-occupied Singapore 1991*, Tynron Press.
17 a Transcribed sermon from Saint John's Review 15 (January, 1948): p 20.

Rome, but it was a plan of bringing eternal life to those who would put their faith and trust in Him.

Why else would the early Christians walk bravely into an arena where they knew were there to execute them? Why else would those early disciples, on the way to be burned at the stakes, sing songs of praise? It was because they were convinced that evil and pain had suffered defeat through what God had done on that cross of Calvary and the resulting Resurrection. Death was not the end. That's why the Christian church has looked at suffering not as an absolute evil, but as an evil that had been conquered by their Lord and Savior, Jesus Christ. For the present time in this world, the evil could be used to discipline them, refine them, into a deeper spiritual life.

To be certain, the Christian does not need to be worried that suffering in the world makes belief in God impossible. It is only belief in a suffering God that stops us from either becoming totally callous or becoming insane at all the suffering that afflicts our world.

2. The Problem of Emptiness

The problem of emptiness is really not just a problem for the poor, or the uneducated. It is a universal problem, because a feeling of meaningless can strike an affluent physician, to a "rescue mission alcoholic." It can even strike the "religious, church going" person. It seems that the longer I am in ministry, the more I realize how this problem of a lack of purpose and meaning is prevalent. This problem is stated in a variety of ways:

- "We came from nothing, and we go to nothing."

- "I make all this money, but am I really that much happier?"

- "How come I am never satisfied with my successes, or my material things?"

The problem of emptiness was illustrated to me after a church service. After everyone had gone home, I went into my office and found a note. It read like this:

> *Dear Pastor, My life is a mess. I know that much of the problems I have brought on myself, but why do I feel so empty. I have a lot to be happy about. I have a great job where I make really good money. I have a beautiful wife and some great kids. But it seems that lately, I'm not happy! I feel running away! I feel restless. I came to church for the first time today in a long time. You don't know me, and I don't really know you. But right now, I am so down that I can't possibly see any daylight. I know my wife feels the same, though we don't talk about it. Maybe I just need to leave for awhile. I've gone to several bars and massage parlors, but do not seem to find fulfillment. I mentioned I have great kids, but I just can't seem to get close to them. I feel alone and without much hope. Help. ????*

This story reminds me of one of the wealthiest men who ever lived. His name was King Solomon. In his search for fulfillment and meaning to life, he became very wealthy.

One day he looked at all he owned, and his <u>beautiful house</u> with <u>elaborate gardens</u>, and he said, "*I denied myself nothing my eyes desired; I refused my heart no pleasure. My heart took delight in all my work, and this was the reward for all my labor. Yet when I surveyed all that my hands had done and what I had toiled to achieve, everything was meaningless, a chasing after the wind; nothing was gained under the sun*" (Ecclesiastes 2:10-11).

In another portion of scripture, he tried to live the <u>party life</u>. He said, *"I thought in my heart, "Come now, I will test you with pleasure to find out what is good." But that also proved to be meaningless. "Laughter," I said, "is foolish. And what does pleasure accomplish?"*

I tried cheering myself with wine, and embracing folly--my mind still guiding me with wisdom. I wanted to see what was worthwhile for men to do under heaven during the few days of their lives. (Ecclesiastes 2:1-3)

On another occasion, he tried being a <u>workaholic</u>, and found the same emptiness. *"I undertook great projects: I built houses for myself and planted vineyards. I made gardens and parks and planted all kinds of fruit trees in them. I made reservoirs to water groves of flourishing trees.* (Ecclesiastes 2:4).

But the Bible gives us a completely different path towards happiness. According to the scriptures, true happiness is never something that should be sought directly. It is always the result of seeking something else. Please think about this: When we are trying to be happy, we rarely find it. But when we forget about those things and get back to the purpose for which God has placed us on the earth, we find true long lasting happiness. That's when our lives have balance.

God has designed us to understand that apart from Jesus Christ, we are spiritually destitute. Regardless of our bank account, or our education, or our accomplishments or even religious knowledge, it all leads to empty vacuum. In my lifetime, the most terrible illustration that I ever viewed of a person feeling like there is no hope was a man by the name of R. Budd Dwyer.[18] Budd Dwyer, was a former Pennsylvania politician, who committed suicide at a press conference January 22, 1987, live on Television. He proceeded to give out letters to his staff, which contained

---

18 Fortunecity.com/Budddwyer

private information, then took a gun and shot himself on live television.

I am not saying that everyone who struggles with emptiness will end in up like Budd Dwyer. Yet, there is a sense of hopelessness or a 'treadmill" feeling about life, when the tasks that we do each day, do not lead to a singular purpose.

If you have bought into this philosophy of life, of course you won't find any sense in any this God talk. But it is a chicken and egg situation. And I would remind you, one can only live with this feeling of emptiness for a period of time before life becomes too much. The atheists answer is to deny God or ignore Him, and then see if you can make sense of everything else. The fact is… <u>you can't</u>!

But try it the other way around. What if there is a God? Then the world is not merely a coincidence. It is the result of His creation. Humanity is not incidental, but we are stewards of this earth and the Gospel. , but God's deputy on this earth. If God does exist, and He is loving and gracious as the Bible presents, then, In this scenario, the Budd Dwyer's of the world would find forgiveness, and hope. I challenge anyone to find a reasonable philosophy that gives meaning, and that provides forgiveness and hope for the future.

3. The challenge of Proof

The third problem is the question of "proof." Some say, "You can't prove God," And that's true. But there are a lot of things in life that you can't prove. And if you think about it, they are usually the most interesting areas of our lives – such as proving someone loves you, or why something is beautiful to one person, while not beautiful to another. The problem is in the very definition of "proof." Most people, when they use that term, talk about it as a final word of certainty. Yet, this type of *proof* is only applicable in very few areas of life. Still, most of the time, we make final decisions based on good, credible evidence without actually having proof.

One of my favorite shows is CSI Las Vegas. And in each episode, the CIS team searches out the evidence and makes conclusive reasoning based on the evidence. My point is that there are good reasons (evidence) for believing in the existence of God. In fact, there is more evidence for the existence of God then evidence that he does not exist. I would qualify this statement by saying that though it may not be conclusive proof, it provides rational reasons why it is much harder to reject the existence of God, than to accept that He doesn't exist.

Below are several factors to consider.

Consider the Law of Cause and Effect

As far as we know at present, there is no other life in any other part of the universe. So, why is there life here? Why did the Big Bang *theory* center on this planet verses other planets? Think about it. This planet is the only part of the universe where there is human life. This world cannot just exist out of chance. The reason it can't is because at every turn is the issue of cause and effect. It isn't rational to believe that something of chance with the complexities of our world can actually birth a world of physical laws that have been built on "cause and effect." Think about it. The car that I drive had to be made by someone. The house that I live in was built by some builder. We are the product of a cause and effect world. Therefore, if everything around me is an effect who or what caused it? For me, there is very little evidence for chance. There is a greater amount of evidence that God was the cause. If you really look at the world, and how everything works (cause and effect) then science itself will make you think that the first cause had to be an intelligent architect - the Creator.

Intelligent Design

Wherever you look in nature, there is evidence of an intelligent design. Let me give you several examples from the world that creates a problem for evolutionists in this who area of intelligent design.

The Bombardier Beetle is a rather interesting one. When threatened this beetle a fluid known as *benzoquinones* from two nozzles at its back end. This fluid is secreted from the body at a temperature of 212 degrees Fahrenheit. The expulsion of the fluid is the result of the mixture of hydrogen peroxide/hydroquinone solutions mixing together inside the beetle. So as not to mix them together, the chemicals are kept inside two separate chambers. When this beetle secretes the fluid it actually shoots it out in various bursts. If it shot out in one blast, it would propel the beetle backwards [19]. The point is that evolutionists have a hard time explaining the complexities of this beetle.

Another example of God's creativity is the "woodpecker." It has a very thick and tough beak which enables it to peck into the trees to find food. If an ordinary bird would try to do that it would break its beak. So, it is impossible for an ordinary bird to evolve a woodpecker's beak after many years of pecking trees. Also, think of the "two toes in front" and "two toes in the back." This assists the woodpecker in climbing and grasping the tree. In the European Green Woodpecker, the tongue runs from the back of the skull beneath the skin and over the top between the eyes, terminating just below the eye socket. Evolutionists cannot

---

19 Martin, Jobe, D.M.D., Th. M.; *The Evolution of a Creationist*, [Rockwell: Biblical Discipleship Publishers, 2005], p. 39.

come up with an explanation of the uniqueness of this bird.[20]

But the question is still as follows: If there is a design in the world, where did it come from? The answer: Not from us. Modern Physics has gone a long way toward reinforcing this suspicion with the *Anthropic Principle.* This principle suggests that the world looks very much as though it has been designed for human beings to live in it. If things were only slightly different, life would be impossible. If gravity was stronger, we would not be able to move. If gravity was weaker, we would fly off the ground!

I believe that this is one of the strongest arguments for the existence of God. To shut one's eyes to this reason would be to deny a rational persuasion. Psalm 19:1 states it clearly, "*The heavens declare the glory of God; the skies proclaim the work of his hands.*"

The Trait of Personality

This factor states that there is a fundament difference between a person or a thing. We are not robots, and there is more to us than a programmable machine. The <u>fact</u> that there is some type human personality points to a causative figure. We do all have personality! And as a result, I am to relate to others who have the same mechanism of personality. I am more than just a thing. The fact that there is human personality brings to the surface the fact that it is more reasonable to believe intelligent design than not

The Presence of Ethics

The fact that there is "conscience" or "ethics" points to an intelligent designer. Think about it this way: your

---

20 Michael Denk, *Intelligent Design: Proof of Creation*, "February 2007, Catholic Family News"

conscience is a lawgiver that lives inside of you. It either acquits you or condemns you. It is a warning signal to you. But this warning signal is affect by several things:

It is warped by our environment – if you grew up in an abusive family, then you may be able to believe that "physical abuse" is acceptable in certain cases. It can also be warped by our rationalization – President Bill Clinton's statement when he was in office regarding whether a certain type of sexual practice was regarded as sexual is a great example of the type of rationalization which can warp one's conscience. Finally, it also is warped by our disobedience – Sometimes we just plain enjoy being bad. We know that a certain practice will hurt us or even others, but we just want and love doing it! But know this, that conscience can't just be explained away as the pressure coming from society. In fact, society many times approved of a certain type of behavior from slavery to bigotry.

No. the presence of conscience and ethics are not issues which are derived from chance. You don't have to be a Bible Thumping Fundamental Christian to realize that there are some things which are absolutes. For instance, ask yourself (whether you are an atheist, agnostic or whatever) the following questions:

1. Is adultery right or wrong?
2. Is murder right or wrong?
3. Is torture right or wrong?
4. Is lying right or wrong?

C.S. Lewis summed it up like this: *"If no set of moral ideas were better than another, there would be no sense in preferring civilized morality to Nazi morality. The moment you say one lot of morals is better than another, you are in fact measuring them by an ultimate standard"*[21]

---

21 C.S. Lewis, *Mere Christianity* (HarperCollins, 2001.

No – ethics, morality, and conscience, and the difference between right and wrong, are important indicators of a God who is interested in what is right and wrong, good and bad. He is a personal God, who is so concerned with what is right, that he has built a moral gauge into each one of his creatures.

General Acceptance of Religion

We are religious animals. From the beginning of time to the present, people have attempted to abolish religion. Yet, they failed. Put aside this book, and that I am an evangelical Christian and realize that from the jungles of South America to our own nation in America, there is a desire to worship something. Some worship nature. Others worship idols. Still others worship Jesus. But the point is that there is inside every human being the desire to worship something.

Conclusion

These facts taken together not only make belief in God reasonable, but also make it very hard to rationally deny God's existence. They point to a God who is skillful enough to design creatures in the earth to even the development of a baby. They point to a God who is the source of human personality and is personal. He is the ultimate source of our values. He is also so concerned about right and wrong that he has furnished each of his creatures with a conscience.

My challenge to those on the other side is to answer this chapters theme. Can evolution or any "child" of evolution answer….

1. The issue of Anthropology?
2. The problem of Meaninglessness?
3. The problem of Suffering in the World?
4. The origin of personality?
5. The existence of morality?

6.   The universal appeal of religion through the centuries?

Frankly, I am bored by those who say they believe in evolution, but "only" deal with partial explanation for the universe (the scientific part only!). They are great in bringing up questions but when they are confronted with explaining their position with the paradigm given in the above chapter, they are at a loss. They lean on the questions of science only, while ignoring other areas of consideration. Many of the arguments brought by evolutionists stay only on the physical evidence or their interpretation of the evidence.

But, reasonable people recognize the complexity of humanity. My challenge for you, the reader is to open up your mind to see that intelligent design answers more questions than evolution ever could. So far, what do you think? Which argument is more reasonable? Which is a more rational approach to the existence of a personal God?

But if God exists. Which God is it?

- Is the Christian (monotheistic – one God) view of God correct?

- Or Is the Buddhist (pantheism – everything is god!) view God the correct one?

- Maybe the Hindu (polytheistic – many gods) view of God is the path to take in understanding who God is?

In the next few chapters, there is a controversial subject which will be discussed. It is controversial because of the claim that Christ makes in John 14:6, and other passages. In John 14: 6, Jesus said, *"I am the way, the truth and the life. No man comes to the father, but by me."* Now, if Christ is the only way, where do all the *other religious paths* stand in the grand scheme of it all?

Chapter Three

Do All Religions Lead To God?

Having dealt with the *deification* of Science and some of the evidence for intelligent design (God), allow me to focus on the issue of Christian exclusivity. Can smart people believe in a singular God, and can one really identify Christ to be the only Savior of the World. I can only imagine what some of you are saying. I recognize that it sounds prideful and seemingly arrogant. That is not my attitude. But religion, for the sake of the reader, I am defining it as man-made rules and attempts to reach ultimate heaven without a Savior. I am defining Christianity as a belief in a personal God who created the Universe and who sent his Son (Christ) to be the only Savior of the World. And this same Jesus has made, what some may call the arrogant statement – John 14:6 says, *"I am the way, the truth and the life. No man comes to the father but by me"*. A true follower of Christ leaves no room for vagueness in this issue. From a Biblical perspective, there is one God, and His Son is Jesus the Christ who is the only Savior of the world.

Think about it. This religious all inclusive attitude has become so appealing to the world that we are sacrificing truth. And to become dogmatic about anything has become nauseating. In fact, anyone who claims exclusivity is looked upon as intolerant, and even biased.

I think there are three reasons why people get very upset when, in religious discussions there is a claim for exclusivity. First, there is the problem of political correctness. Ever so often in the news there are children's coaches and leagues that believe we should take out competition from children's athletics. We hear absurd comments like, "Don't worry little suzy that we lost the game. Or little Johnny, we don't keep score anymore in the games, we don't want to hurt the other team's feelings." This attitude that we don't want to be looked upon by others in a negative light has spilled over into religious discussion. Let's not offend. Please understand, that I am not a radical fundamentalist. I'm all for weighing our words and respecting each other, but sometimes the truth is hard to take, but we need to hear it. If there are two sets of truths presented, one can be wrong and the other right. The second reason why I think there is such a desire for blending all religious faith, is due to a "fear" of religious fundamentalism whether it comes from the Middle East or from America. We used to wear proudly the badge of the "ugly American." I grew up in the 80's and remember the pride when the USA won the Olympic gold in Ice Skating. The chanting of USA, USA, USA echoes in my mind of growing up in a country that was proud. Now it seems that the goal is to compromise, and even up the field of play for fear that some evil terrorist is going to be upset that a religion (Christianity) can claim exclusivity. In the words of Ed Rendell, the Governor of Pennsylvania when the city of Philadelphia cancelled the Eagles and

Vikings game, *"We have become a nation of wusses!"*[22] So, I'm an anti-wuss because I <u>do</u> believe that Christ's sacrifice is the extreme picture of love for all mankind, and there is no other path. The third reason I think people get upset is because until a few years ago many universities taught courses in Comparative Religion and it was a course very few students actually took. But the world is getting smaller. Other major religions are becoming more publically known. For instance, just a few years ago, Hinduism, Buddhism and Islam were regarded to be on the fringe of society. Further, students who have become disenchanted with Christianity are turning to these religions for the answers to the major questions of life. That is understandable.

Therefore, on the basis of these three reasons it is imperative that we should ask the following questions.

- Can you really distinguish between all these religions?

- Are all the religions the same?

- Don't all roads lead to God, and if so, picking one may not be as hard as you might think?

The Indian leader Mahatma Gandhi once said: "*The soul of religions is one, but it is encased in a multitude of forms... Truth is the exclusive property of no single scripture. I cannot ascribe exclusive divinity to Jesus. He is as divine as Krishna or Rammer or Mohammed or Zoroaste.r*"[23] Is Ghandi right? Can we really place all religions on an even platform and ignore the differences? My position is that this view is unreasonable for two reasons.

---

22 Washington Post. "*Ed Rendell – We have become a nation of Wusses.*" Editorial page, December 28, 2010.

23 R.K Prabhu and R.R. Rao, <u>The</u> Mind of Mahatma Ghandi, Greenleaf Books, 1988.)

It is unreasonable

It may feel good to believe that all religions are basically one. But unfortunately, this thought is false. "How can all religions lead to God when they come from such different perspectives?" Take for instance, the god of Hinduism which is either atheistic or polytheistic. While the God of Christianity is singular and personal.

On another perspective, Christianity teaches that God forgives and gives us a new life and forgiveness. But in Buddhism, there is no forgiveness and no spiritual help. The goal in Buddhism is to reach a "nirvana," a tranquil extinction – which is only achieved by the Buddha after 547 births. Christianity says, *"We are confident, I say, and would prefer to be away from the body and at home with the Lord"* (2 Corinthians 5:8). When it comes to marriage, Islam allows bigamy (four wives), while Christianity allows for one. Yet, perhaps the greatest difference of all lies between the teachings of the Bible (Christianity) that assert that none of can save themselves and make themselves pleasing to God. But Isalm, Budhhism and many other religions are self achieving realizations. They hope that through their belief system, a person can either be saved, reborn, made whole or achieve fulfillment.

I found an article by Earnest Valea entitled "*The Parable of the Prodigal Son in Christianity and Buddhism*" [24]in a web site (comparativereligion.com) which quotes from the Buddhist writings, *Saddharmapundarika 4*. This source contains some of the earliest writings of the Buddhist beliefs and actually presents one of the most powerful contrasts of a well familiar Biblical story – the story of the *prodigal son*. In the Buddhist version, the son comes home after

---

24 Earnest Valea, "*Parable of the Prodigal Son in Christianity and Buddhism*" comparativereligion.com.

spending all of his wealth foolishly and is met by the father. In this Buddhist version he has to work off the fine or the penalty for his past indiscretions by serving his father for a number of years. The principle of _Karma_ (*paying off your guilt*) is very much different from the Christians' view of *grace* (forgiveness when you don't deserve it at all). In the Christian version, the father pays off the debt. Christ is the one who pays for our guilt and sin, as we (incapable of paying our own sin) depend on His sacrifice.

I do not want to make this section an evaluation of different religious faiths. I just want to show you how _illogica_l it is to say that they are all pointing in the same direction.

Back in 2009, my family bought me a GPS for Christmas. It is probably one of the best investments that my family has made. What I have found is that there are a number of similar named cities in America. For instance, Danville, Pennsylvania is also in Danville, California. It would silly to punch in Danville in my GPS without the state and expect to get to the right location. All roads do not lead to Danville. It is not helpful to _pretend_ that they do for the sake of being regarded as _open-minded_. For they in fact, lead to radically different locations.

You name it. Whether it is soul annihilation vs. a Literal Heaven; Or it is a complete pardon for sins vs. paying it off (*Karma*); or it is a personal vs. impersonal god, the contrasts are conflicting!

The trouble is that today's tolerance has reached a point where it is no longer a virtue, to stand on principle, but it is looked upon as a weakness.

It is in my opinion that those who believe that all religions lead to the same goal are either academically Blinded or scholarly lazy. The point being that there is a casualness to truth. Think about it. There are lawsuits when "truth" and "facts" are overlooked in the medical field.

Would you go to a doctor who would overlook cancer in your body for the fear of making another doctor look bad or you feel hurt! It is not right to ignore the facts for the sake of unity in the world. We are simply showing ourselves to be cruel if we say to a blind person who is sitting on the edge of a cliff that it doesn't matter which way he moves, because all paths lead to the same goal. It is equally illogical to place all religions on the same footing.

The End is Coming or Is it?

Second, I also believe that the differences among religions are accentuated through their belief on the end of time. Most religions view history in a cyclical motion. There is a cycle of birth, growth, and death through which all creatures and humans pass. And this cycle is continues on and on. The end time paradigm for Christianity is more focused. This is the view of both Judaism and Christianity. History needs to be seen as a long voyage. Christianity and Judaism is very much different in their belief of end times. The other point I would make is that in both these religions (Christianity and Judaism) believe in a final judgment. In other words, God will come onto the earth and all mankind will be held ultimately accountable for their stewardship of this earth and of His gospel. That is why the historical accounts of both lead to heaven.

My point is that it is very inconsistent to the facts and truths to conclude that all religions travel the same road.

But why specifically is it impossible for us to find God among all the religions of the world? Let me give you two reasons:

Why Can't We Find God in the World's Religions?

God is Infinite

When someone uses the term "God," usually he is describing an entity who is infinite and above His creation. He isn't a part of the creation. He is separate from it. One day when Job had been arguing with God, He rebutted Job's complaints with a reminder that God was God, and job was just a man. *"Where were you when I laid the earth's foundation? Tell me, if you understand. Who marked off its dimensions? Surely you know! Who stretched a measuring line across it (Job 38:4-5)?* Then, in the book of Isaiah, God elaborates the same thought as of Job.

> *Do you not know? Have you not heard? Has it not been told you from the beginning? Have you not understood since the earth was founded? He sits enthroned above the circle of the earth, and its people are like grasshoppers. He stretches out the heavens like a canopy, and spreads them out like a tent to live in. Whom did the LORD consult to enlighten him, and who taught him the right way? Who was it that taught him knowledge or showed him the path of understanding? Surely the nations are like a drop in a bucket; they are regarded as dust on the scales; he weighs the islands as though they were fine dust.* (Isaiah 40:21-22,14-15)

The idea that somehow we can become like gods, or attain godlike qualities is a ridiculous statement - wishful thinking, maybe. In fact, name a person in modern history that has attained that characteristic of controlling nature or the elements. Wait a minute! I can give you a name. Jesus.

35

- Jesus walked on water- *"Come," he said. Then Peter got down out of the boat, walked on the water and came toward Jesus"*. (MT 14:29)

- Jesus stilled an ocean storm - *He replied, "You of little faith, why are you so afraid?" Then he got up and rebuked the winds and the waves, and it was completely calm."* (MT 8:26)

- Jesus healed the sick *—Jesus turned and saw her. "Take heart, daughter," he said, "your faith has healed you."- And the woman was healed from that moment.* (MT 9:22)

- Jesus Fed the hungry - Then he took the seven loaves and the fish, and when he had given thanks, he broke them and gave them to the disciples, and they in turn to the people. They all ate and were satisfied. Afterward the disciples picked up seven basketfuls of broken pieces that were left over. The number of those who ate was four thousand, besides women and children. (MT 15:36-38)

When I think of God, that is precisely what I look for in a God. And to think that some religions believe that you can have those qualities within you, is beyond reason.

Yet, there is a second reason why man is incapable to make his own path to God. Not only because God is infinite, but also because man is sinful, and finite

Man is Sinful

Throughout the Biblical scriptures mankind is not pictured in great terms. For instance, look at the following Biblical statements:

- The Bible says that, we are not good as we believe ourselves to be. In fact, we are pretty self-centered and sinful. Colossians 1 says *"We are alienated from God and were enemies in your minds because of your evil behavior."* (Colossians 1:21)

- We are out in reality without control. I've heard people say that we should always follow our hearts, yet the bible says, *"The heart is deceitful above all things and beyond cure. Who can understand it?"* (Jeremiah 17:9) Following your heart can lead to unplanned pregnancies, abortions, and all types of rationalizations for doing evil things.

- We are deceived at how bad it is to sin against God. In other words, we are blinded into thinking that God "dislikes" sin, rather than actually hating it. Romans 1 says, *"The wrath of God is being revealed from heaven against all the godlessness and wickedness of men who suppress the truth by their wickedness,"* (Romans 1:18)

- Fourth, we actually love sinning. John 3 says that *"Men love darkness rather than light because their (our) deeds are evil"* (John 3:19).

Patrick Lawler was an individual who thought he had a toothache. For almost a week, he tried painkillers and ice packs to reduce the swelling. When nothing he did brought relief, he finally went to the dental office where his wife works. Only after the dentist took THIS X-RAY did Patrick learn the true source of the toothache. He had a four-inch nail in his head. When the dentists reported their discovery to Patrick's wife, she thought they were joking. But the x-ray revealed the truth. The nail had entered through his mouth, just missing Patrick's right eye. The incident occurred six days earlier. Patrick was working with a nail gun that backfired. One of the nails shot into his mouth and embedded itself, but Patrick didn't realize it. He merely complained of a toothache and blurry vision, and even tried ice cream to soothe the pain. After the nail was discovered, surgeons at a Denver hospital successfully removed it through four hours of surgery. Although it is a rare injury one neurosurgeon admitted, "...this is the second one we've seen in this hospital where the person was injured by the nail gun and didn't actually realize the nail had been embedded in their skull."[25] The point is that he thought that he had a bad tooth ache, and all he needed was some dental work. Yet, this guy needed major surgery.

The same problem exists in the spiritual realm. We feel we are not "that" bad. Our marriage may be falling apart, or we are hooked on an addiction, but we gloss over it as mere indiscretions or a mistake. Yet, those are only symptoms of a deep seeded issue of sin and forgiveness. We need God to perform major surgery on our lives in order to cleanse us from sin. Then and only then will the symptoms get better.

The lie of society is that "we are good people down deep in our hearts, and if we have enough time, we will all be ok." This is foolishness. If that is true, why does crime keep going up in our nation. And even in places that it goes down we get all excited because it dropped a percentile or two. Only to see two years down the path that crime has gone up again. You can throw as much money at education we will still have a failing society. Jesus pinpointed the problem when he said, *"Everyone who sins is a slave to sin"* (John 8:34).

---

25 MSN.com/pattricklawler, January 21, 2005.

No wonder the Paul comes to the same conclusion that the Old Testament had reached when he said, "*None is righteous, no, not one; no one understands, no one seeks God*" (Romans 3:10-11).

Think of it this way: The infiniteness of God and human sinfulness are two massive issues thinking that all religions lead to God. They do not.

Where is the Source of Encouragement?

Since there is <u>no</u> way for man to reach God due to the GREAT DIVIDE between the Infinite and finite, what then is left?

God needed to reach make a path for us and the Bible provides for us the manner that He did it.

God Unveiled Himself

If you were God, and you had a group of people who did not follow your path and they were disconnected from their creator, what would you do? Let me tell you what God did by taking you through a historical journey of the Christian faith.

In Genesis 11, God decided to begin his quest for the hearts of the world by selecting one individual by the name of Abraham. Abraham, for the most part was very obedience to God. He trusted God, and in turn God made him the father of the Jewish people. Yet, the nation of Israel rebelled from God's relationship with them. As a result, God allowed hardship in the hands of the foreign countries with the hope that they would humble themselves and turn once again to Him. This was in the era of Joseph where they spent much of their time in slavery during the Babylonian Captivity. He then sent prophets like Isaiah, Jeremiah and Ezekiel to warn them of their rebellion. Jeremiah 25 said, "*And though the LORD has sent all his servants the prophets to you again and again, you have not listened or paid any attention."* (Jeremiah 25:4) Finally, God loved mankind so much that he didn't just send an angel or a trusted prophet, He sent His very Son. And each year, millions of people celebrate His birthday at Christmas. The worship the one called Jesus, who has been given the title of *"Emmanuel"* ("God with us").[26] For the moment that God the Father sent His son, we were introduced to a personal loving God. God was no longer the unknown God. For Jesus who became a man was able to feel and understand the plight of humanity. And so, God revealed himself to us.

God Saves Man

Yet, the coming of Jesus did not merely show us what God is like. It also showed us what we are really like. The apostle John wrote, *"Men loved darkness rather than light, because their deeds were evil,"* (John 3:19). Just take a glance at the newspapers and you will see the extent of worldwide depravity of mankind. In each newspaper article there is a clear understanding that we do love darkness rather than light. As a result, the human race needed something more basic even than a <u>revealer of God</u> . We needed a <u>Savior</u> – one sent by God. Do you understand the two purposes of Jesus' coming? It was a pronouncement that God loves humanity, but the fact that He had to send His son, was also a pronouncement of our sinfulness and our inability to be good enough or do enough good works to get to heaven. That's what Christ accomplished when he died for our sins. He put us right with God by his sacrificial death. That is why the cross is the symbol of Christianity. It is the

---

26 MT 1:23 "The virgin will be with child and will give birth to a son, and they will call him Immanuel" --which means, "God with us."

most important achievement in all of history. For on the cross Jesus, the God-Man, took responsibility for human sin. Peter state it this way: "*For Christ died for sins once for all, the righteous for the unrighteous, to bring you to God. He was put to death in the body but made alive by the Spirit*" (1 Peter 3:18). The apostle John agreed: "*This is love; not that we loved God, but that he loved us and sent his Son as an atoning sacrifice for our sins*," (1 John 4:10).

The Christian Experience is Unique

I've attempted in this chapter to help you understand that to make the statement, all religions are the same, is rather foolish. For the Christian experience is unique. In the book of Revelation, which gives us a glimpse into the future, there is a scene where God gathers from all parts of heaven those who have put their faith in Christ. They begin to cry loudly. "*After this I looked and there before me was a great multitude that no one could count, from every nation, tribe, people and language, standing before the throne and in front of the Lamb. They were wearing white robes and were holding palm branches in their hands. And they cried out in a loud voice: "Salvation belongs to our God, who sits on the throne, and to the Lamb*" (Revelation 7:9-10).

Do you see the uniqueness of Christianity? For Jesus came to reveal God's heart, but He also came to save us from a sin, that has rendered us incapable of saving ourselves (through religion).

No other religion can have that claims. Whether you speak of the "goodness" of Ghandi or the protective power of Allah they all fall short of the redemptive aspect of Christianity. None can speak of the type of the sacrifice of leaving heaven and dying for the sins of the world.

Please understand that I am not saying that there are not "qualities" of those other religious experiences which are _not_ beneficial. I believe all truth comes from God, and truth is truth. So then, there are elements of Islam which coincide with the truth of God's word such as honor and goodness to fellow man. There are good elements to Judaism and Buddhism etc. But I am saying that you will not find the <u>redemptive qualities</u> for man in any other religious experience than in the story of Jesus. His story is very unique.

But the question still lingers: Why? Why would God make such a horrific sacrifice by placing His Son on the cross?

God's Purpose in Sacrificing His Son

To my surprise, he wants to have a relationship with us. In fact, the resurrection of Christ is what enables us to have an eternal relationship with God. In fact, the News testament lays out carefully the documented evidence of the resurrection of Christ, because that is the ultimate proof of his deity. And it is through the resurrection that we can worship not a dead hero of the faith, but a risen Lord and Savior of the World.

I am a Pastor and in my last church we had a tradition where I would lead the communion service and usually one of my Assistant Pastors would help me in passing the elements of the "Bread" (representing the broken body of the Lord), and the "cup" (representing the blood of Jesus) which was shed on the cross for our sins. And so, we usually had a chair for me and for my Assistant Pastor. But we usually had a third chair. And it again was representative, because in the Pauline account there is a statement which stated that the act of communion will only be practiced until Jesus comes again. For when Jesus comes, there will be no need to practice the Lord's Supper. *For whenever you eat this bread and drink this cup, you proclaim the Lord's death <u>until he comes</u>* (1Corinthians 11:26). The point is Jesus is alive and he wants to relate to his created beings.

No other religious practices does that. For Christianity is very unique in comparison to all the other religious experiences.

CHAPTER FOUR

Is the Bible Trustworthy?

The Bible is very important to me. But sometimes I feel that it's really hard to get people to believe in it. It is very much like trying to set up singles on a date. When I was in college, I had a good friend who was rather dateless throughout our years at Philadelphia College of Bible (now, Philadelphia Biblical University). I also was good friends with a girl who was in my Bible class. Well, it would be appropriate for you to start singing: *"Matchmaker, Matchmaker, give me a match. A perfect Match!"* But my problem was getting them together. Both of them were great people! He was a great friend, and she was a great looking girl. And they would have made a wonderful couple. The problem was that they were both shy! In fact, my friend was real quiet, especially around girls! It was actually interesting to notice that their first meeting was an awkward and uncomfortable time for both, to say the least. And…surprise, surprise, surprise? They didn't get married. They both are happily married today, so I'm glad I didn't go into the matchmaking business.

But in many ways, that's how it is to introduce *some* people to the Bible. For many, it is a date that feels awkward because it takes place in the Middle East, and in a language that you can't fully understand. Further, it just seems old fashion. They observe society and believe that the Biblical World View is incompatible to the real life that we live during this 21ˢᵗ century.

Let's discuss, first of all, the various approaches to the Bible, that people take.

Various approaches to the Bible

The Inkblot Approach

Most people approach the Bible like the inkblot test. This was is a psychological test back in the 1960's in which subjects' perceptions of inkblots are recorded and then analyzed. The Interpretation was at the subject's preference. Many people approach the bible with that type of perspective where the Scriptures are not held to a single interpretation, but instead it should be read with whatever meaning we want to impose on it. They tell us that no single interpretation should be considered objectively valid. Most postmodernists would state it this way: *"Any biblical text has a life of its own – and once it is written, the reader provides the meaning."*[27] This approach to the bible has natural dangers, which my lead to "weird" conclusions about life, death and the eternity.

The Pick and Choose Approach

Another approach to the Bible is to regard "portions" of the Bible as irrelevant, while accepting some of it.

---

27 Alex McFarland and Tony Campolo. Adventures in Missing the Point. Zondervan: El Cajon, California. P 269.

Recently, I was talking to a person from our hometown Lewisburg, Pennsylvania. He was sharing with me, how the parts of the Bible that he has disregarded involved the sections where certain moral judgments are made about people's lifestyle. When I pressed him about specific questions, he shared with me that he was still married, but living with a woman he met online. He further felt that homosexuality was not sin, and that immorality outside of marriage was ok as long as people didn't get hurt. Then, strangely, he shared the parts of the Bible that he liked. He loved the story of Jesus in a manger, his miracles, and even the death/resurrection story. As the discussion continued, I mentioned the following verses and asked him, "since these verses are no longer for today, should we physically cut them out of the Bible?" His response was that these verse still had historic value. But my question remained, "On whose authority or what other portion of scripture can we with great assurance cut these verses out and put them into the category of scriptural irrelevance?"

- EX 20:14 "You shall not commit adultery.

- LK 18:20 You know the commandments: 'Do not commit adultery, do not murder, do not steal, do not give false testimony, honor your father and mother.' "

- 1CO 6:9-10 Do you not know that the wicked will not inherit the kingdom of God? Do not be deceived: Neither the sexually immoral nor idolaters nor adulterers nor male prostitutes nor homosexual offenders nor thieves nor the greedy nor drunkards nor slanderers nor swindlers will inherit the kingdom of God.

My contention is that the reason why these verses are labeled "irrelevant" because the lifestyle that we are living is in direct opposition to those verses. It is easier on our conscience to disregard than to engage ourselves in change.

Unreliable Approach

A Third approach to the Bible is to disregard the scriptures as unreliable and filled with mistakes. This objection is revolved around several criticisms. One criticism states that the Bible is full of mistakes after thousands of years of copying and translating. Skeptics usually echo the thought, "Surely, there must be a book or two that wasn't intended to be a part of the Bible." Another objection, within the same lines, is that the Bible is such an *old book* it <u>must</u> have errors in it. The fact is that the <u>age of the Bible</u> and the <u>content of the Bible</u> are two completely different issues. Antiquity does not automatically imply error.

In this chapter, I want to give you some facts, and provide evidence why the Bible is trustworthy, and is reliable in every challenge.

Ancient Manuscripts and the Bible

Many believe that in tracing the reliability of the Bible is extremely difficult because much of the manuscripts were dictated on reed papyrus and parchment skins, then they were rolled into various scrolls. Since everyone did not have access to these writing elements a high regard was placed on hearing the scriptures. It wasn't until 1456 that Guttenberg invented the printing press and printed the first copy in Latin. The work of scribes was meticulously done as they understood that the very words of God were being dictated. In some cases when errors were found, the entire copy was destroyed.[28]

---

28 Biblemuseum.net/VirtualHistory/The History of the Bible, Part 2.

The earliest copy of the Old Testament, called the "Masoretic Text" can be dated around 900 A.D. The word "Masoretes" literally means "transmitters." From A.D. 500 to 1100, they were careful writers of the Old Testament. It is amazing to understand the process that they took to make sure that the Greek/Latin version the Hebrew Old Testament was correctly translated.[29] In fact, as theologians read this ancient manuscripts and compared it to the Qumran Dead Sea Scrolls it was remarkably the same.[30]

In 1947, an archeological find was found to be eye opening. In caves, along the Dead Sea, ancient Jars were found containing what is now known as the Dead Sea Scrolls. The scrolls were the product of a group of scholarly egg heads called the *Essenes*. They lived in an area called "Qumran from 150 B.C to A.D. 70. They were mostly monastic and spent much of their time studying and copying the Word of God. This discovery was magnificent because it yielded eleven jars full of scripture. It contained the entire book of Isaiah, as well as the book of Esther, the books of Samuel and two complete books of Habakkuk. The reason why this find was so remarkable is because it brought down the span of reliable texts 1000 years.[31]

Three Old Testament Versions deemed Reliable

Due to wars, the Jewish people had to move to different parts of the world. As a result, various translations have been found from Egypt to Rome. The three most famous translations are the *Septuagint*, the *Syriac* version, as well as the *Samaritan* versions.[32]

29 Alex McFarland. *The 10 Most Common Objections to Christianity*. Regal Books: Ventura California, 2007. p. 81.
30 Wikipedia.org/wiki/masoretic_tex
31 Alex McFarland. *The 10 Most Common Objections to Christianity*. Regal Books: Ventura California, 2007. p. 82.
32 Paul E. Little. Know Why You Believe.IVP Books: Downers Grove, IL. p 77..

The *Septuagint* means "seventy," and is the Greet translation of the Old Testament. It is the oldest translation. This translation was actually done by way of Alexander the Great who wanted to Hellenize the world. It was translated by seventy two Jewish scholars in 3 B.C.[33]

The *Syriac* version was written in the Aramaic language. It is Syrian as the name implies. This translation was prominent after the Septuagint. The *Samaritan* version came as a result of a split between the Jerusalem Jews and the Samaritan Jews but again it was regarded as reliable.[34]

New Testament Versions Variations Minimal

Author	Date Written	Earliest Copy	Time Span between original & copy	Number of Copies	Accuracy
Plato	427-347 BC	900 AD	1200 years	7	----------
Aristophanes	450-385 BC	1200 AD	1200 years	10	----------
Aristotle	384-322 BC	1100 AD	1400 BC	49	----------
Homer	900 BC	400 BC	500 years	643	95%
New Testament	1st Century (50 -100 AD)	2nd Century (c. 130 AD)	Less than 100 years	5600	99.5%

Figure 1: Variations sampling[35]

F.J. A Hort who is a great scholar who once stated that, "*the New Testament documentary evidence is remarkable*

---

33 Ibid., p 78-79.
34 Ibid., p78-79.
35 Josh McDowell, Evidence that Demands a Verdict. Here's Life Publishers, inc: San Bernadino, California, 1979.

because when comparing the various documents there are only a few variations in grammar or spelling between them.[36]

It is said that there are over 5,600 manuscripts n of the New Testament alone. Some are complete books, while others are only sections of scripture. In Figure 1 (above) chart it shows the remarkable reliability as compared with Other historical documents which are rarely if ever challenged.

Other Sources deem the Bible Reliable

Authenticity of the bible can also be seen in other areas. The historical documents from Christianity's enemies such as King Herod and Pilate all collaborate the story of Jesus. Cornelius Tacitus is a name that most will not recognize, but he has given to this chapter an enormous boost in confidence on the reliability of the New Testament. He lived during the time of the 1st Century Church (AD 90 – 130). It is also important to note that Tacitus was not a follower of Christ. He was born in France into an aristocratic family. He became a Senator and a Governor of Asia, but is more well-known for being a historian. Around 115 AD, he wrote his *Annals*, which was an accounting of the fire in Rome (64 A.D. in which Nero had set and then blamed it on the Christians. A huge persecution occurred during that period of time and many Christians died at the hands of Nero and his soldiers. It was in that context that he wrote about a man named Christus, who had been put to death by Pilate.

Consequently, to get rid of the report, Nero fastened the guilt and inflicted the most exquisite tortures on a class hated for their abominations, called Christians by the populace. Christus, from whom the name had its origin, suffered the extreme penalty during the reign of Tiberius at the hands of

---

36 B.F. Wescott and F.J.A. Hort, eds, New Testament in Original Greek, vol 2 (London 1881), p 2.

one of our procurators, Pontius Pilatus, and a most mischievous superstition, thus checked for the moment, again broke out not only in Judæa, the first source of the evil, but even in Rome, where all things hideous and shameful from every part of the world find their centre and become popular. Accordingly, an arrest was first made of all who pleaded guilty; then, upon their information, an immense multitude was convicted, not so much of the crime of firing the city, as of hatred against mankind. Mockery of every sort was added to their deaths. Covered with the skins of beasts, they were torn by dogs and perished, or were nailed to crosses, or were doomed to the flames and burnt, to serve as a nightly illumination, when daylight had expired. world find their centre and become popular. Accordingly, an arrest was first made of all who pleaded guilty; then, upon their information, an immense multitude was convicted, not so much of the crime of firing the city, as of hatred against mankind. Mockery of every sort was added to their deaths. Covered with the skins of beasts, they were torn by dogs and perished, or were nailed to crosses, or were doomed to the flames and burnt, to serve as a nightly illumination, when daylight had expired.

> Nero offered his gardens for the spectacle, and was exhibiting a show in the circus, while he mingled with the people in the dress of a charioteer or stood aloft on a car. Hence, even for criminals who deserved extreme and exemplary punishment, there arose a feeling of compassion; for it was not, as it seemed, for the public good, but to glut one man's cruelty, that they were being destroyed.[37]

---

37 Complete Works of Tacitus. Alfred John Church. William Jackson Brodribb. Sara Bryant. edited for Perseus. New York. : Random House, Inc. Random House, Inc. reprinted 1942.

Josephus, a Jewish historian[38] (about 93 AD) gives much detail concerning the life of Christ, as well as his followers (i.e. gospel writers - Matthew, Mark, Luke and John). Josephus writes:

> *About this time came Jesus, a wise man, if indeed it is appropriate to call him a man. For he was a performer of paradoxical feats, a teacher of people who accept the unusual with pleasure, and he won over many of the Jews and also many Greeks. He was the Christ. When Pilate, upon the accusation of the first men amongst us, condemned him to be crucified, those who had formerly loved him did not cease to follow him, for he appeared to them on the third day, living again, as the divine prophets foretold, along with a myriad of other marvelous things concerning him. And the tribe of the Christians, so named after him, has not disappeared to this day.[39]*

What about the Canon?

The "canon" is a group of books that are in our Bible. Have you ever wondered why some books are a part of the Bible, while others are not? It is important to first note that In the Old Testament, the term "scripture" usually meant a _written_ body of truth communicated by God through human agents. Two illustrations come to mind early in the Bible's history. First, it comes through the biblical character of "Moses." He was given a physical tablet containing the written version of the Ten Commandments.[40] The other was when Nehemiah

---

38 Flavius Josephus, Josephus Antiquities.18.3.3.
39 Wikipedia.org/history of Jesus
40 Exodus 20

who was rebuilding the city of Jerusalem found the scripture. Imagine, for the very first time in centuries Ezra, the prophet read from it in Nehemiah chapter eight.[41]

It is certain that from the very beginning there was a clear focus on what was considered to be scripture and what was not. It wasn't until the Church Council of *Jamnia* in A.D. 90 that a formal list of scripture was suggested. To be certain, that about 397 A.D. a New Testament canon was formalized.

We are grateful to a letter written by *Athanasius* in A.D. 367 where he provides three criteria for making the determination what books should be a part of the Canon. The three were as such:

- Were the writings authored by an Apostle?

- Were the books generally recognized as scripture by the Early Church?

- Was the teaching of the book consistent with the standards sound doctrine as preached in the early church?

The Apocryphal Books Not in the Canon

The word "apocrypha" means "concealed." It consists of seven books which were excluded from the Protestant and Jewish Bibles. In the late fourth century it was seen in a Latin Translation of the Old Testament, but later it was challenged by church fathers such as Jerome.

The books of the Apocrypha has never claimed inspiration (God Breathed) nor were they authored by any of the prophets. During the time of the reformation it was challenged by Luther and many others. That is why the Roman Catholic Bible includes these books, while the current post-reformation Bibles have deleted them.

---

41 Nehemiah 8

The point is that the written scriptures were extremely important throughout history. That is why I Evangelicals have a very high respect on the authority of God's Word the Bible in its original writings.

With this background information, I am sure that there will be a number of challenges and questions that is beyond the scope of this book. There are a couple of questions that need to be answered. First, w*hy do Evangelical Christians make such a big deal of a literal view of the Bible?*

A little while ago I had a discussion with a student about how in their campus, it is very acceptable that after a party students "hook up" with those of the opposite sex. This type of free sexuality is prevalent in our culture and in secular campuses. There seems to be no embarrassment because some students actually post it on social networks for all to see, so they obviously do not see anything wrong with it. When I pointed out to this young student that the Bible regards it as sin, he began to shake his head in disagreement. After I finished my little homily, he said, *Pastor Ruba, this is your interpretation.*" So, I asked him, "Tell me how would you interpret the words, *"Flee from sexual immorality. All other sins a man commits are outside his body, but he who sins sexually sins against his own body"* (1 Corinthians 6:18). He then proceeded to argue the fact that "no one" lives that way! I am 50 years old and grew up in the 60's and 70's – in fact, hooking up is as old as time. But somehow there is a culture that has made this activity very acceptable, and they have been convinced that it is unique. As not to digress, allow me to share on this issue of interpretation scripture and cultural practices.

First, I do not hold a "strict literal view of Scripture." A strict literal view approaches every figure of speech, and every portion of scripture, literally. Take for instance this passage from Deuteronomy: *"If brothers are living together and one of them dies without a son, his widow must not marry outside the family. Her husband's brother shall take her and marry her and fulfill the duty of a brother-in-law to her"*(Deuteronomy 25:5). A strict literalist would take this passage literally, and so if my brother died and they did not have a son, I would by Biblical grounds, be commanded to take my brother's wife. But this passage needs to be taken in light of the culture, the literary genres, as well as the historical and textual context. I would mention that passages like this one are not at all common. Most of the time, the authors of the books were very forthright in their statements. Interpretation of each passage starts with an "exegetical" understanding of the passage. The term "exegesis" refers to getting the meaning out of the text, rather than imposing a meaning that was not intentional. It was explained to me back in Bible College that every verse is connected to a chapter, which is connected to a book of the Bible, which is part of the whole historical framework of the Bible. In real estate the three most important items are location, location, location. In Biblical interpretation it is context, context, context.

Second, it is very dangerous to approach scripture from the framework of what is acceptable in our society. In reading various historical writings it is amazing how "slavery" was defended and preachers, as well laity back in the Civil War era, misused the scriptures. Even some today defend the "white supremacist" positions as Biblically sanctioned. Our starting point needs to be the scriptures. Why? Let me share some passages of scripture. *"All Scripture is God-breathed and is useful for teaching, rebuking, correcting and training in righteousness, so that the man of God may be thoroughly equipped for every good work"* (2Timothy 3:16-17). All scripture is God-Breathed (Inspired), and useful for teaching, rebuking, correcting and training with the end result of being fully equipped. *"For the word of God is living and active. Sharper than any double-edged sword, it penetrates even to dividing soul and spirit, joints and marrow; it judges the thoughts and attitudes of the heart"* (Hebrews 4:12). This passage says that the Word of God is a living document. It gets to the root of our problems. That is why when people come to me, as a Pastor for counseling, eventually we wind up in the Bible, because opinions come and go. My opinion and perspective is still just another man's opinions. But if you take God's Word literally you begin to understand that there is authority behind those words. It IS the WORD OF GOD!

How then should I interpret Bible Passages?

To my young friend who seems to excuse his view of "hooking up," I would challenge him to study the Bible and interpret it like any other book. Allow me to give you some tips or rules for interpreting the scripture correctly. But let me preface it by saying that there are entire college and seminary courses dedicated to this subject alone. But here are some tips that will help you in making good sound interpretations.

> *Tip #1 Always interpret the Old Testament in light of the New Testament taking in the context of the writings. As who, what, and why.* Remember that the New Testament always gives light to the Old Testament passages. (As a side-note, that is how you answer the Deuteronomy passage!)

> *Tip #2 Scripture always interprets Scripture. Refuse sloppy interpretation.* Dig in. Find out the context of the passages, as well as the history behind the issues. Study

the etymology of the word (the historical development of words).

Tip #3 *Pray and ask God to give you an answer to the problem text.*

Tip #4 *Do not make it more complicated than it actually may be.* Last time I noticed, a command is really a command. If God says, "Don't do something," then realize that it means "Don't do it!" Now, isn't that easy?

Tip #5 *Take the Bible seriously.* Have the confidence that if you live according to God's Word, it will bring a peaceful life here on earth as well as praise from heaven.

I am a Pastor, and please understand that people who have very "complicated" relationships and lives I believe are people who have looked at the Bible; picked and chosen which commands they will obey or not obey. Adultery in a marriage brings the possibility of divorce. Lying and cheating brings dismissal from schools and jobs. Uncontrolled Anger can lead to all sorts of abuses.

It is my desire that, at least those in my own congregation would live "uncomplicated' lives. It is my desire that you, the reader, would live an "uncomplicated life." It begins with having a high view of Scripture, and follows it up with a high view of obedience.

Missing the Main Point of the Bible

Now, one the greatest danger in this chapter is for you the reader to believe that the Bible is God's Word, and yet miss the main point of the Bible.

For the point of the Bible is to point you and me to Christ. Think of it this way:

1. The Old Testament looked to the future of the coming of the Messiah (Jesus, the Christ).

2. The New Testament Gospels (Matthew, Mark, Luke, and John) give witness that Christ was the Son of God, and that He is the Savior of the World.

3. Then, the rest of the New Testament is written to tell people what it means to live a life committed to Christ.

Yet, many people, in approaching the Bible look at it as a list of do's and don'ts, or words to comfort in time of great need, but they miss the main point of the Scriptures. In fact, when Christ was on earth, he confronted this very subject of believing the scriptures, while some at the same time were missing the point. For in John chapter 5, and verse 39, *Jesus said: "You diligently study the Scriptures because you think that by them you possess eternal life. These are the Scriptures that testify about me, yet you refuse to come to me to have life"* (John 5:39-40). Jesus is talking to the Pharisees, who were students of the Holy Scriptures, and they memorized big sections of the scriptures, but Jesus is saying to them, "You've missed the main point!" He is saying, "Don't stop at just *appreciating* the Bible, for the main purpose of the Bible is to lead you to put your faith in Christ and to provide eternal life. That's the end goal!

Howard G. Hendricks is a great teacher from Dallas Theological Seminary. This is what he said about not missing the main point of the Bible.

The Bible was written not to satisfy your curiosity but to help you conform to Christ's image. Not to make you a smarter sinner but to make you like the Savior. Not to fill your head with a collection of biblical facts but to transform your life.[42]

Howard Hendricks is correct! Some of you who are reading this book think that by going to Sunday School, and reading a Bible verse or two, or being kind to your neighbor will be sufficient to getting you to heaven. Please understand that the Bible has great amount of wisdom to give us. And you *should* go to Sunday School and read the Bible and be kind to your neighbor. Al of that is beneficial.

But don't miss the <u>main</u> point! And the main point is that Jesus wants you and me to place our faith in Him for the forgiveness of all our sins. The Bible is written to point people to Christ, the only one who can forgive sins, and give a life eternal in heaven.

That is why *if* you call yourself a Christian you then are inferring full allegiance to Christ and at the same time you are turning away from other religious figures/philosophies. Christ did not leave any room for a mixture of religious practices and formulas. He stated in John 14:6, *"I am the way, the truth and the life. No man comes to the father but by me."*

---

42 DailyChristianQuote.com/*HowardHendricks*

CHAPTER FIVE

Is Jesus the Only Way to Heaven or is Oprah right?

If there is one thing that people do not want to hear is that the real nice guy down the street who works in the soup kitchen during the holidays; who goes to church; and who is real committed to his family, may not be going to heaven.

We don't like to offend people, especially when it comes to matters of eternal significance. We would love to think that everyone we meet is going to heaven. In fact, our society tends to elevate inclusiveness, not exclusiveness. We don't like to talk about judgment or hell, because, again… we cannot fathom a loving God punishing "nice people." That's why many times, Evangelicals (the "born again" type Christians) are called "narrow minded and bigoted." Yet, the scriptures are pretty emphatic about some who are going to heaven and some who are going to hell. The only argument rests on the basis of how one may get there.

Society's approach is to be completely inclusive. And the only way for modern society to include everyone is by fashioning their own type of God, who accepts all, and who has no absolutes. Truth is sacrificed in the altar of unity.

This type of Christianity tends to ignore basic Biblical teaching and in some cases reject completely certain passages of Scripture. This type of "water down" Christianity is all around us. For example, almost <u>eighty percent</u> of all people believe that there is more than one way to heaven. <u>Ninety One percent</u> of Catholics agree with this view. And probably the most telling is that <u>sixty eight percent</u> of "Evangelical Christians" believe that a good person, from another religion will go to heaven.[43] And on top of that, 65% of evangelical teens say you can't be sure which religion is right! [44] If those statistics are true then there are a lot of people who do "not know" clearly what the Bible teaches.

Now, the problem *cannot* be attached to atheism because many of the surveys cited do show that a high percentage of people consider themselves to be "spiritual." The problem is that they have chosen an I-pod version of the Bible (choose our own mix) rather than understanding what the Scriptures clearly state. This has also been called the "salad bar" religion where we mix and match what we want to (eat) believe.

This is where 'Oprah" comes into this book. She grew up with a Baptist background, but according to *Christianity Today,* she seemed to have picked and chosen those aspects she deems true. Her show has a variety of "Spiritualist" leaders, Gurus, and various New Age authors. I must admit that she is a great humanitarian, and she does a lot of good with her money,[45] But the question still rests on whether

---

43 *Newsweek National Poll of 1004 people www.beliefnet.com.*

44 *Lee Weeds, "Teens No Sure Christianity is the Only Way," Pulpit Helps* (January 2001).

45 Christianity Today, *The Church of O,* April 1, 2002

all her good works will "earn" her a place in heaven? I will answer that later!

Maybe a little recapping of what we've already studied in this book will help in answering this question. So far, we've recognized four essential truths.

1. God is real.

2. God created the world and man.

3. God initiated communication with us through the Bible and it is reliable and accurate.

4. All religions are not alike and do not all lead to Heaven.

But, now we have to answer this question of, *"Is Jesus the only way to heaven?"* Or is Oprah Winfrey correct with her "salad bar approach?"

Allow me to answer it this way. Christianity does not leave room for an inclusiveness type of salvation such as was described earlier in the book. In other words, there are <u>not</u> many ways to God. Jesus has not made a secret of this truth. In John 14, we read:

Jesus answered, "I am the way and the truth and the life. No one comes to the Father <u>except through me</u>. (John 14:6)

Later, Jesus made this statement which I am sure raised some eyebrows.

"All things have been committed to me by my Father. No one knows the Son except the Father, and no one knows the Father except the Son and <u>those to whom the Son chooses to reveal him</u>." (Matthew11:27)

"You are a king, then!" said Pilate. Jesus answered, "You are right in saying I am a king. In fact, for

this reason I was born, and for this I came into the world, to testify to the truth. Everyone on the side of truth listens to me." (John 18:37)

For my Father's will is that everyone who looks to the Son and believes in him shall have eternal life, and I will raise him up at the last day." (John 6:40)

I tell you the truth, he who believes has everlasting life. (John 6:47)

Just as Moses lifted up the snake in the desert, so the Son of Man must be lifted up, that everyone who believes in him may have eternal life. "For God so loved the world that he gave his one and only Son, that whoever believes in him shall not perish but have eternal life. For God did not send his Son into the world to condemn the world, but to save the world through him. (John 3:14-17)

I give them eternal life, and they shall never perish; no one can snatch them out of my hand. My Father, who has given them to me, is greater than all; no one can snatch them out of my Father's hand. I and the Father are one." (John 10:28-30)

Jesus said to her, "I am the resurrection and the life. He who believes in me will live, even though he dies; and whoever lives and believes in me will never die. Do you believe this?" (John 11:25-26)

"Whoever acknowledges me before men, I will also acknowledge him before my Father in heaven. But whoever disowns me before men, I will disown him before my Father in heaven. (Matthew 10:32-33)

Maybe you have never really thought it through but all these passages are rather exclusive! They paint Christ to be the ONLY way to heaven, and other ways as leading to eternal punishment. And so, who is right? The exclusive words of Jesus Christ? Or the mix and match religion of Oprah? Who is right?

Where's the Beef?

Back in 1984, *Wendy's Restaurant* put together a Television Advertisement starring an older lady who received a bun from fictional competitor which used the slogan *"Home of the Big Bun"*. The small patty prompts the older lady to say angrily, *"Where's the beef?" And that is a great place to start in answering this question.*

"Ok, Jesus! If you are the exclusive one that people should look for salvation, give us your evidence?"

Now, when Jesus claims that He is the _only way_ to salvation (John 14:6), or the _sole gatekeeper_ of heaven, we must evaluate that claim against everything we know of Christ. For I believe that when we do that, if we were to reject Christ that would require more faith, and much less reliance on logic, history, and experience than simply accepting Jesus at His Word.

For Jesus wasn't just pulling His material out of thin air. His life demonstrated it. His resurrection confirmed who He was and what He taught. And by His coming back to life, He proved beyond a shadow of doubt that He had every right to not only "boast" in His heavenly Father, but also to claim Himself as the only way to eternal life.

Various Views of Jesus

Throughout history, there have been skeptics and believers who have argued about the historical Jesus. Here are five different views that you and I can choose from, but please base your choice on sound Biblical reasoning. Your eternal destiny rests on making the right choice.

1. Some see Jesus as merely a _Myth_: This view was popularized by a British philosopher named Bertrand Russell who made claims that "Jesus was simply an element of folklore."[46] He viewed Jesus as a legendary, fictitious character whose life was made up by a lower class culture as an emblem of hope. So, in many ways he was a batman type of individual who was made up to give hope to the poor.

2. Then, there are those who see Jesus as a mere _Man_. If we accept the premise that Jesus did in fact exist, this view claims He was simply a human with a God-complex. There have been a number of people throughout history that have been deluded into thinking that they are "a messiah type." One such person in my lifetime was a man by the name of Jim Jones. His ull name was _James Warren Jones_, and he was the founder of People's Temple. I remember the day that Jim Jones and his 900 members of his church, in Jonestown, Guyana committed mass suicide. I remember it because I was a freshman at Philadelphia College of the Bible where many students prepare for full time missions or church ministry vocations. On November 18, 1978, Jim Jones and his 900 member church committed mass suicide by drinking "cool aid" mixture of poison.[47] Also, five other people died

---

46 Drew.edu "_Why I am not a Christian._" Lecture originally given in 1927
47 Wikipedia.com/Jim Jones.

in a nearby airstrip trying to leave, including United States House of Representative, Leo Ryan from the 11th congressional District of California. Maybe Jesus was a Jim Jones type of person – Very charismatic, influential but very dangerous.[48]

3. Maybe Jesus was a *Mystic*: Some New Age followers hold Him up as a guru. They note that much of Jesus' life is unrecorded in Scripture. They state that these "unrecorded" years –– were devoted to journeys to India.[49] This view holds that the followers of Jesus were overwhelmed by Jesus' teaching and as a result they invented the Miracles for the sake of universal appeal.

4. A fourth view of Jesus is simply called, *Misrepresentation*: Some believe that Jesus was a scheme invented by the church to control people. Maybe Jesus, after his death, was made into this superhero by the church so as to create enthusiasm and financial gain for the organization. An example of this is

5. A fifth view is that Jesus was the *Messiah*: That's the money question of this chapter. For as long as Jesus is considered just another human being, it's impossible to make sense of his mysterious life and death. But once Divinity is established and accepted everything changes. For one thing, if Jesus is indeed God in human form then all of His miracles can be explained by His power. But more to the point- if Jesus is indeed

48 Wikipedia.com/Leo Ryan.
49 Bahktivedanta Wasmi Prabhupada. *Bahkta Handbook*: harekrishnatemple.com/ Chapter 27 on line book.

God, then we have no choice but to follow him and to accept that he is "*the way, the truth, and the life*" (John 14:6).

Now, if you've read this far into the book, it should come as no surprise to you when I say that I believe Jesus is God. He is the Messiah and the Savior of the world.

So, the question before us is this: On what grounds do I draw this conclusion? For anyone can walk into a room and claim to be from the PLANET *NANO NANO*. But for people to really take you seriously you better be able to prove it. You better explain how you came to earth, and you have better show evidence. Our tendency, though, is to believe what we can only see.

This was recently brought to my attention by 30 year old skeptic of Christianity. The film by *Bill Maher* had just hit the movie theatres, and Christianity was on the chopping block of a lot of critics of the Bible. At the time I had not viewed the film, but seriously, anything coming from Bill Maher just seemed foolish, if compared to some of his other gripes about society. I just don't get his humor! Yet, he has voiced some issues which need to be addressed, because of my skeptic's objections to Christianity.

Bill Maher – Intellectually Dishonest

Bill Maher's major problem with Christianity is that the entire New Testament is made up. Furthermore, he would state that the stories in the New Testament are not even original. He goes to great lengths in his movie *Religulous*, to state that there were stories from the Mediterranean area for at least 1000 years that contain accounts almost identical with the New Testament accounts of the life of Jesus. In his movie, *Religulous,* Bill Maher accuses Christian leaders that they have plagiarized the story of Jesus. He cites three historical individuals –who are Krishna, Mithra, and Horus. Krishna (approximately 1000 B.C.) is seen as a god from the Far East who was a carpenter, born of a virgin mother, and was baptized in the river. Mithra , who lived around B.C. 600, was a mythological god who was born on December 25th and, performed miracles. He was also attributed to have risen from the dead on the third day. Then, there was Horus. He was also regard as a god in the *Egyptian Book of the Dead* dated at 1280 B.C. Horus had 12 disciples; and was crucified and died. Reportedly two women visited him after 3 days, and testified that Horus was resurrected from the dead and is the Savior of Humanity.[50]

Without getting too technical and losing the point of this chapter, Krishna's supposed dating was incorrect. There are no writings of him in 1000 BC, but Bill Maher misread the date because he is not mentioned until <u>A.D.</u> 1000. Mithra has no written sources. It has been rejected by scholars. And Horus has no Egyptian records to back up these claims.

I would cite former atheist, but now Christian apologist, Lee Strobel, in his best-selling book entitled, "*The Case for Christ.*" Lee Stobel states firmly that, "*all the books of the New Testament were written within <u>70</u> years of Christ's death and resurrection, and probably even earlier than that.*"[51]

I find it interesting that Bill's attacks on Christianity lack educational credibility yet because of his popularity is given authority as an esteemed " intellectual." I am also curious why some educators chose to study this book as part of a High school or College class? That is, while at the same time there is a removal of any element of Christian teaching within the schools. Just a question: Where is the

---

50 adapted from *inspirit.org/Bill Maher Review of Religulous*
51 Lee Strobel, *The Case for Christ.* Zondervan Publications, 1998, Grand Rapids, Michigan: p 57

desire for scholarly integrity when there is so much evidence of Jesus that they would grasp at a poor academic theory by Bill Maher?

Christ's legitimacy rests on His Resurrection

The greatest hang-up to Christ's claims comes to the fact of His resurrection. In the words of "The Pirates of the Caribbean" ride at Disney World – "Dead Men Tell No Tales!" In other words, it is a fact that when you're dead, you're dead! But this brings us to the very heart of the Christ's claim. For Christianity is the only religion of the world to emphatically proclaim that we can know something about what awaits us, for the simple and only reason that Jesus Christ, was crucified and died on the Cross, and arose from the grave.

Now, most skeptics would say that it cannot be true. But can it? The possibility of it really rests on four issues:

1. Was Jesus God? Or Man?

2. Did he predict his own death and resurrection?

3. Was there any credible testimony that He actually rose from the Dead?

4. What other Historical testimony is there to add to the proof of the resurrection?

Let's take time to examine the evidence.

1. Was Jesus God or Man?

One of the first questions that most skeptics point out is that "*Jesus never said that he was the Son of God!*" And that is absolutely true. He never said those *exact* words as recorded in the Bible. Yet, I would mention that am not personally surprised by that!

Christian apologist Lee Strobel interviewed Ben Witherington (Professor of New Testament at Asbury Theological Seminary in Kentucky), and asked him basically the same question, namely, "Why did Jesus never come out and say he was God?[52] Here is Witherington's response:

"The truth is that Jesus was a bit mysterious about his identity, wasn't he?" I asked, as Witherington pulled up a chair across from me. "He tended to shy away from forthrightly proclaiming himself to be the Messiah or Son of God. Was that because he didn't think of himself in those terms or because he had other reasons?" "No, it's not because he didn't think of himself in those terms, Witherington said as he settled into his chair and crossed his legs. "If he had simply announced, 'Hi, folks; I'm God,' that would have been heard as 'I'm <u>Yahweh</u>,' because the Jews of his day didn't have any concept of the Trinity. They only knew of God the Father–whom they called Yahweh–and not God the Son or God the Holy Spirit. " So if someone were to say he was God, that wouldn't have made any sense to them and would have been seen as clear-cut blasphemy. And it would have been counterproductive to Jesus in his efforts to get people to listen to his message. "Besides, there were already a host of expectations about what the Messiah would look like, and Jesus didn't want to be pigeonholed into somebody else's categories. Consequently, he was very careful about what he said publicly. In private with his disciples–that was a different story, but the gospels primarily tell us about what he did in public."[53]

Let me summarize for you. For Jesus to say that he was God would have meant to the people in the culture of that day, that he was claiming to be the ***same Person***

---

52 Strobel, *The Case For Christ* [Zondervan Publishing House; Grand Rapids, MI, 1998 - Pocket Size Edition], pp. 178-.
53 Ibid., p 179.

commonly referred to by both Jews and Christians as the **_Father_**. Yet Jesus was not the same Person as the Father, but was personally distinct from him, although sharing the same essence and nature with him. So, Jesus did not say the words, "I am God!", but he certainly made claims that would characterize him in that fashion.

Jesus Claimed Equality with God

First, Jesus did claim equality with God, the Father. One of Jesus' clearest statements came in response to the Jewish leaders' question: The Jews gathered around him, saying, *"How long will you keep us in suspense? If you are the Christ, tell us plainly."* Jesus answered, *"I did tell you, but you do not believe. The miracles I do in my Father's name speak for me, but you do not believe because you are not my sheep. My sheep listen to my voice; I know them, and they follow me. I give them eternal life, and they shall never perish; no one can snatch them out of my hand. My Father, who has given them to me, is greater than all; no one can snatch them out of my Father's hand. I and the Father are one."* (John 10:25-30)

In opposing Jesus' statement of "I and the Father are one", some theologians have interpreted it that Jesus wasn't claiming to be God but merely saying that he was a man with great power like God. Yet, if that was true, then why didn't He shed light on his statement when the Jewish leaders had a stone in their hands ready to kill him. Further, they said in John 10: *"We are not stoning you for any of these,"* replied the Jews, *"but for <u>blasphemy</u>, because you, as but a man, claim to be God."* (John 10:33). That makes sense, doesn't it! If someone stood over me and said, "Rubens, I think that you are Pavarotti. You sing and He sings. You are from another country (Brasil) and He is from another country. Then with a gun pointed at my head they would ask me, "Are you really

Pavarotti? I would have to say, "No, I was just kidding." So it was with Christ except He didn't back down because His statement stands firm in his testimony.

What did Jesus then mean when He said that He was one with the Father? The Jews understood "the Father" to be their Creator/God – God the Father (Deuteronomy 32:6; Isaiah 64:8). For Jesus wasn't implying that He and the Father were the _same_ person, but that He and the Father were of the same _nature_. They were equal in rights, authority, privileges, and power. So, in effect, Jesus was saying that He had complete and sovereign power over their lives - a claim that enraged the Jewish leaders.

In another occasion Jesus asked the disciples, _"Who do you say that I am?"_ (Matthew 16:15) And after a few names were thrown out of what others believed Jesus pressed them. _"Who do you say that I am?"_ And Peter replied, _"You are the Christ, the Son of the living God"_ (Matthew 16:16). Jesus did not correct Peter but actually commended him for his answer. He said, _"Blessed are you, Simon son of Jonah, for this was not revealed to you by man, but by my Father in heaven."_ (Matthew 16:16)

Jesus Claimed Divine Authority

Second, throughout the gospels, Jesus declared His deity through His claims of authority. He announced the following:

- He forgave sins (Mark 2:5); only God can forgive sins. Of course, the Pharisees understood the implication He was making and again wanted to kill Him for such a blasphemous remark (Mark 14:64-65).

- He called himself "I AM" – which placed him in equality with Jehovah God of the Old Testament (John 8:58).

- He announced that he was the Messiah (Mark 14:61-64)

- He even encouraged people to pray in His name (John 14:13-14).

- Finally, He identified Himself as the Savior of the world (John 3:16; 6:29; 7:38).

Jesus Did What Only God Can Do

Look at some of the miracles that He performed throughout his ministry life on earth

- He healed people. (Matthew 9:35; 11:4)

- He calmed the storm (Mark 4:35)

- He fed thousands of people. (Mark 8:1-9)

- He showed His power of spirit beings. (Mark 1:27; Luke 4:1-13)

- He passed that miracle working authority onto His disciples. (Matthew 10:1)

So then, Jesus identified himself as deity, claimed divine equality and backed that claim up with authority over life, death, illness, and the spirit world.

2. Did Jesus predict His death?

Now, this question is very critical to this discussion. Did Jesus actually predict his own death and resurrection? Let me share with you that just six different times that Jesus predicted not only his death but his resurrection.

From that time on Jesus began to explain to his disciples that he must go to Jerusalem and suffer many things at the hands of the elders, chief priests and teachers of the law, and that <u>he must be killed</u> and on the <u>third day</u> be raised to life. MT 16:21

- I would equate this statement, if I would predict my own death and say that, "I am going to die in *Philadelphia*, and a fierce gang named the Rubenites are going to be the people responsible for my death." But then I said, "don't worry, in (not one or two) but three days later I will come up out of the grave." That is pretty specific and verifiable.

When they came together in Galilee, he said to them, "The Son of Man is going to be betrayed into the hands of men. <u>They will kill him</u>, and on the <u>third day</u> he will be raised to life." And the disciples were filled with grief. MT 17:22-23

- One thing that we notice here is that the disciple apparently believed Jesus' prediction, because *"they were filled with grief."*

They were on their way up to Jerusalem, with Jesus leading the way, and the disciples were astonished, while those who followed were afraid. Again he took the Twelve aside and told them what was going to happen to him. "We are going up to Jerusalem," he said, "and the Son of Man will be betrayed to the chief priests and teachers of the law. <u>They will condemn him to death and will hand him over to the Gentiles, who will mock him and spit on him, flog him and kill him. Three days later he will rise.</u>" MK 10:32-34

- Here's something else to think about: How did he know that he would flogged?

Jesus took the Twelve aside and told them, "We are going up to Jerusalem, and everything that is written by the prophets about the Son of Man will be fulfilled. He will be handed over to the Gentiles. They will mock him, insult him, spit on him, flog him and <u>kill him</u>. On the <u>third day</u> he will rise again." LK 18:31-33

- We can look back and see the fulfillment of this prediction that they would *"mock and spit"* on him.

And he took bread, gave thanks and broke it, and gave it to them, saying, "<u>This is my body given for you;</u> do this in remembrance of me." In the same way, after the supper he took the cup, saying, "This cup is the <u>new covenant in my blood, which is poured out for you</u>. LK 22:19-20

- This statement was made the night before his death. Again, another prediction of his death.

Was the evidence Jesus actually rose from the Dead?

This centers on the very action of Christ's Resurrection. It strikes at the testimony of each Gospel writer. Here are four questions of Jesus' death and resurrection which need to be explained in order for this question to be answered.

- **<u>Jesus' burial</u>** – was Jesus actually put into a tomb and with it, was he dead and in it?

- Was the tomb empty?

- **<u>His post-mortem appearances</u>** – Was there credible testimony given by reliable witnesses?

- **<u>The origin of the disciples' belief in his resurrection</u>** – If the resurrection did occur, did it have a profound effect on his disciples? Let me share with you four facts which correspond to the issues stated above.

The empty tomb is a witness

There were multiple eyewitnesses that Jesus died and they buried him in a tomb, while putting a stone in front of it. We have four biographies of Jesus by <u>Matthew,</u> <u>Mark,</u> <u>Luke,</u> and <u>John</u>, which give the written testimonies to Jesus' death and resurrection. The Apostle Paul as well gives his account along the road to Damascus (the place where he spoke with the resurrected Jesus. Let me point out that the Gospel of Mark is the earliest source of information which gave eyewitness accounts. Many historians date the Gospel of Mark on seven years after the crucifixion. The Apostle Paul's account was probably written no more than five years after the Crucifixion. Moreover, Paul also cites an extremely early source for Jesus' burial which most scholars date to within **five years** of Jesus' crucifixion.

Another grouping of evidence comes from the discovery made by the women early on Resurrection Day. In Jewish society , a woman's testimony was <u>considered credible</u>. In fact, the Jewish historian Josephus says that women weren't even permitted to serve as witnesses in a Jewish court of law. (Masada: Josephus, *Jewish War7*, 399). Now in light of this fact, it is amazing that the Lord would allow women to be the first discoverers of his resurrection. The only rational reason is that, even though they were not regarded as the best witnesses, the scriptures are not going to leave the facts. And the fact was that they WERE the first at the tomb, and societies' biases should never compromise the truth.

In examining the evidence, it would be easy to argue with individual witnesses because most of them would be alone at the sighting of Jesus in His resurrected state. An analogy would be, "if I witnessed a spaceship coming down at 3am, and I was the only one present at that citing, you could relate that citing to the pork and sauerkraut I had the night before. But the evidence does not stay with just individual witnesses. And some of the witnesses were not followers of Christ. They were against Jesus. For instance, Jesus appeared to Peter and the Twelve Disciples (1 Corinthians 15:5. He then appeared to a group of 500 disciples at once (1 Corinthians 15:6). Finally, he appeared to his younger brother James who apparently was not a follower of Christ. (1 Corinthians 15:7).

Some people have brought the accusation that the Resurrection of Jesus as just a big Hoax. When asked this question, Chuck Colson responded in this fashion. This is what he said in his radio commentary show called "Breakpoint" back in 2002.

Watergate involved a conspiracy to cover up, perpetuated by the closest aids to the President of the United States—the most powerful men in America, who were intensely loyal to their president. But one of them, John Dean, turned states evidence, that is, testified against Nixon, as he put it, "to save his own skin"—and he did so only two weeks after informing the president about what was really going on—two weeks! The real cover-up, the lie, could only be held together for two weeks, and then everybody else jumped ship in order to save themselves. Now, the fact is that all that those around the President were facing was embarrassment, maybe prison. Nobody's life was at stake. But what about the disciples? Twelve powerless men, peasants really, were facing not just embarrassment or political disgrace, but beatings, stonings, execution. Every single one of the disciples insisted, to their dying breaths, that they had physically seen Jesus bodily raised from the dead. Don't you think that one of those apostles would have cracked before being beheaded or stoned? That one of them would have made a deal with the authorities? None did. You see, men will give their lives for something they believe to be true—they will never give their lives for something they know to be false. The Watergate cover-up reveals the true nature of humanity. Even political zealots at the pinnacle of power will, in the crunch, save their own necks, even at the expense of the ones they profess to serve so loyally. But the apostles could not deny Jesus because they had seen Him face to face, and they knew He had risen from the dead. The Watergate cover-up reveals the true nature of humanity. Even political zealots at the pinnacle of power will, in the crunch, save their own necks, even at the expense of the ones they profess to serve so loyally. But the apostles could not deny Jesus because they had seen Him face to face, and they knew He had risen from the dead.[54]

Finally, there is the evidence found in the recorded writings of the Early Church Believers. Within the verses of the New Testament are portions that scholars call "creedal statements." Creeds were simply summarizations of Christian beliefs. They were Biblical beliefs passed along, _orally_. The most famous "Scriptural Creed" is taken from 1 Corinthians 15.

Take time to read these carefully. The first creed is seen in a Biblical passage. This creed was regarded as affirming truth for the early church.

1 Corinthians 15 Creed:
Now, brothers, I want to remind you of the gospel I preached to you, which you received and on which you have taken your stand. By this gospel you are saved, if you hold firmly to the word I preached to you. Otherwise, you have believed in vain. For what I received I passed on to you as of first importance: that Christ died for our sins according to the Scriptures, that he was buried, that he was raised on the third day according

---

54 Originally presented on "*Breakpoint with Chuck Colson*" Prison Fellowship Ministries.

to the Scriptures, and that he appeared to Peter, and then to the Twelve. After that, he appeared to more than five hundred of the brothers at the same time, most of whom are still living, though some have fallen asleep. Then he appeared to James, then to all the apostles, and last of all he appeared to me also, as to one abnormally born. 1CO 15:1-8

But throughout history there have been a number of creeds which were designed to summarize and firm up the belief of the church. In all the creeds, the death, burial and resurrection is mentioned. The following creeds are available online at creeds.net.

The Apostle's Creed: (A.D 215)

*I believe in God, the Father almighty,
creator of heaven and earth.
I believe in Jesus Christ, God's only Son, our Lord,
who was conceived by the Holy Spirit,
born of the Virgin Mary,
suffered under Pontius Pilate, was crucified, died,
and was buried; he descended to the dead. On the
third day he rose again; he ascended into heaven,
he is seated at the right hand of the Father,
and he will come again to judge the living and the dead.
I believe in the Holy Spirit, the holy catholic church,
the communion of saints, the forgiveness of sins,
the resurrection of the body,and the life everlasting. AMEN.*[55]

The Nicean Creed: (A.D. 325) Attempted to answer, "Who is Jesus?"

*We believe in one God, the Father, the Almighty,
maker of heaven and earth, of all that is, seen and unseen.*

---

[55] The Apostle's Creed is from the Evangelical Lutheran Church's Web site.

*We believe in one Lord, Jesus Christ, the only Son of God,
eternally begotten of the Father, God from God, light from
light, true God from true God, begotten, not made, of one
Being with the Father; through him all things were made.*

*For us and for our salvation he came down from heaven,
was incarnate of the Holy Spirit and the Virgin Mary
and became truly human. <u>For our sake he was crucified
under Pontius Pilate; he suffered death and was buried.</u>
<u>On the third day he rose again</u> in accordance with the
Scriptures; he ascended into heaven and is seated at the right
hand of the Father. He will come again in glory to judge the
living and the dead, and his kingdom will have no end.
We believe in the Holy Spirit, the Lord, the giver of life,
who proceeds from the Father [and the Son], who with
the Father and the Son is worshiped and glorified,
who has spoken through the prophets.
We believe in one holy catholic and apostolic Church.
We acknowledge one baptism for the forgiveness of sins.
We look for the resurrection of the dead,
and the life of the world to come. Amen[56].*

Who do you say is Jesus?

We began this chapter addressing the question "Is Jesus
the *only* way?" We progressed through the chapter showing
his uniqueness. We ended the last section of this chapter by
showing that Jesus is the only way by virtue of His deity, His
death, and His resurrection. The reasonable and historical
evidence is abundant. So, who do you say is Jesus?

In his book, *Mere Christianity*, C.S. Lewis lists the
options available to us in drawing a conclusion about Jesus.

---

56 Wikipedia.org/Nicean Creed.

The author points out that based on what we know from history, Jesus' true identity is hard to ignore.

> *"I am trying here to prevent anyone saying the really foolish thing that people often say about Him: 'I'm ready to accept Jesus as a great moral teacher, but I don't accept His claim to be God.' That is the one thing we must not say. A man who was merely a man and said the sort of things Jesus said would not be a great moral teacher. He would either be a lunatic - on the level with the man who says he is a poached egg - or else he would be the Devil of Hell. You must make your choice. Either this man was, and is, the Son of God: or else a madman or something worse. You can shut Him up for a fool, you can spit at Him and kill Him as a demon; or you can fall at His feet and call Him Lord and God. But let us not come with any patronizing nonsense about His being a great human teacher. He has not left that open to us. He did not intend to."*[57]

The options that Lewis sets forth: *Either Jesus was a lunatic, a liar, or He was truly Lord.* Yet, I believe that there is a fourth option which some have mistakenly taken. They have seen Christ as a make-believe legend! Bertrand Russell once stated, *"Christ did not exist at all and if he didn't know anything about Him – Jesus is now in the same category as Paul Bunyan!"* [58]

---

57 C.S. Lewis. *Mere Christianity*. The MacMillan Company, 1960, p 40-41.

58 Bertrand Russell, *Why I am Not a Christian* (New York: Simon and Schuster, 1957), p 55-56.

A Historian by the name of *Will Durant* (a Pulitzer Prize Winner and a Presidential Medal of Freedom, identified 19 sources which refer to the Biblical Jesus as a real person. Here are just a few:[59]

- *Thallus* (historian who wrote in A.D. 52 of Christ's crucifixion)

- *Cornelius Tacitus* (Called "greatest historian of Ancient Rome," lived around A.D. 64-116; confirms that Christ "suffered under Pontius Pilate, Procurator of Judea")

- *Gaius Suetonius* (roman historian, wrote in approximately A.D. 120)

- *Emperor Hadrian* (A.D. 117-138)

- *Phlegon* (born A.D. 40 writes in A.D. 140 regarding Jesus' crucifixion and the darkness that occurred at the same time of His death.

- *Plinius the Younger* in A.D. 112 writes about his belief that Jesus was deity!

- *Julianus Africanus* (about A.D. 221; references Christ's death at Passover and the darkness that ensued.

- We also have the famous Jewish Historian, *Flavius Josephus,* the son of Jewish religious leader *Matthius.*

  Josephus was born in A.D. 37, only a few years after Jesus died, and because of where and when he lived, he would have been familiar with the facts about Jesus' life and teachings. Around

---

59 Will Durant. *Caesar and Christ*. Vol. 3 of The Story of Civilization. (New York: Simon Schuster, 1972), p 553-557. Also, online y-jesus. com/Will Durant.

A.D. 67, Josephus began writing as court historian for Roman emperor Vespasian, and almost 30 years later, in Antiquities of the Jews, he comments about Jesus as an actual person.

"At the time lived Jesus, a holy man if He may be called, for He performed wonderful works, and taught men, and joyfully received the truth. And He was followed by many Greeks and Jews. He was the Messiah." [60]

Josephus further authenticated that Jesus was tried by Pilate, accused by powerful Jewish leaders, was crucified and was been alive three days later – 'restored to life.' [61]

I personally hope that you have not lost the point of this chapter. Because from the first century there are historical accounts of a real Man/God named Jesus, and that he died, was buried, and rose again. To deny Christ is to ignore the weight of evidence that points to our Savior. Jesus is real – that fact is verifiable. But again, he's not just a great man in history. Don't be an Oprah! Don't insult Christ by clumping Him in with Buddha or Mohammed. He himself stated these words:

Jesus answered, "I am the way and the truth and the life. No one comes to the Father except through me. JN 14:6

He is the true Son of God, sent by the Heavenly Father to redeem and reconcile all humanity.

---

60 Flavius Josephus, Josephus Antiquities.18.3.
61 Habermas, *The case for the Resurrection of Jesus*, pp 266-270, 284-285

CHAPTER SIX

So What?

I have friends who are in all sorts of fields of study and careers. Some who are teachers, scientists, doctors, nurses, you name it! I consider them very smart people as they are excellent in their perspective fields. And yes, they believe that a personal God exists, the Bible is reliable, and that they need Christ in order to have their sins forgiven.

But I also have other friends, who would put themselves in the category of an agonistic. They believe that there may be (or is) a God, but that's as far as it goes. I enjoy being with them and their families. They are not anti-god, or even anti-Christian. But we do disagree over the reliability of the Bible and the place that Christ plays in their salvation.

Then, there is a very small minority are atheists in the world. I say "small" for two reasons. One, it is statistically proven (check it out) that there really aren't too many of them around. But second, to be honest, I do not really know many atheists. I'm sure they are around but there really isn't too many of them that would be proud of their position and be consistent in there reasoning. Yet, when books are written, they are usually written with them in mind.

That's why this book has been aimed at the first two groups. More than likely, the third group (atheists) will not pick up this book nonetheless "buy it."

Yet, as I set out to write this book, there were really three things that I desired from it. First, is that this book would contribute to encourage open mindedness and dialogue. I mean, true open mindedness where there is a discussion of the key issues, without the stereotypical name calling. My positions are from an evangelical conservative base, but I am not a fanatical non thinking "quiche eater" who cannot argue for my position. And so, let's keep it real and gracious!

A word to _born again Christian_ (of which I am one). Let me encourage you not to be intimidated by the questions that "seekers or skeptics" may throw at Christianity. We do have a reasonable faith.

If you are a _skeptic_ who is questioning faith in Christ, then be the type of person, who reads all perspectives of the subject. The danger is to only get your information from one source, (such as a professor or even a pastor) and then dogmatically close your mind to other views. I am not encouraging a "universalist type of religion," but thoughtful and rational understanding of the issues is always beneficial. As a Pastor and a Christian, the times of questioning my faith have only opened a door to a _deeper_ understanding of God, and His Son, Jesus Christ. As a result, my faith hasn't been weakened. During those times of belief when God was silent, or I've been intellectuality skeptical of one of God's Sovereign decisions, I would testify that they also have been times of tremendous growth. But more than that, they have been times where my faith has actually been strengthened.

Think of it this way. For if God **can't** stand the scrutiny and challenges from a "professor" in a little college or university, is He really that "BIG" and actually <u>worth</u> trusting? Think about it! If God can't stand up to the questions of those who are challenging His Word, and His World View, with their own finite minds, then can He really be trusted with "your life here on earth" or your "life destiny?"

So, please understand that my desire is not to answer all questions. But, I have noticed that there is a "lack of intellectual" openness from those who would categorized themselves as skeptics, and also a "lack of intellectual" interest in Biblical Criticism from those who are believers of Christ.

In the church, there is a tendency to have "quick" answers, and a lack of motivation to study, or to read. This lack of motivation to a deeper faith has added to the false conception that there are NO DIFINITIVE ANSWERS. My prayer is that this book would open doors for your own personal desire to "dig into God's Word." Your eternal destiny rests on your belief system.

Now, there is a second desire that I brought to this book. For I have observed that there is a "demonization" of Christianity in our culture. But it hasn't just occurred with Christianity. It has spilled into anything controversial – politics, parenting, sexual orientation, etc.

There has got to be a better way! Let me illustrate. I am a Republican. And some of you are Democrats and Tea Party members. Further, realize that I have every political party represented in the church that I Pastor - *Lewisburg Alliance Church*, Lewisburg, Pennsylvania? Yet, it is interesting that our rhetoric with each other at church or at meetings does not include "disrespectful or stereotypical" language. " For goodness sake, some of these people live in my neighborhood and our kids have played together in various sports. In fact, I may even disagree on a wide range of issues, not just politics. For out of "dignity and mutual respect," we would never "label" each other, or "create a spirit of disregard for one another's views. Our country needs to bring back a little civility in our discussions of controversial subjects, and this is one of them.

Statements such as "far right or far left" are an appropriate way of identifying our positions. But labeling or stereotyping is wrong. Many times there is a lack of respect in a discussion of religion? I think the reason why we allow this to occur in our society can be summed up in one word: <u>Pride</u>! Somehow, we have equated doctoral degrees and personal accomplishments with wisdom. You can only give your opinion if you have a doctoral degree. Friends, pride is a terrible tool that shuts down thinking, discussion, and debate. Further, pride can come from a person who is a born again Christian who looks down their nose, at the "unbeliever or skeptic." Or it can come from a skeptical administrator or professor in a college University, who uses condescending statements to put down a student. Either way, mutual respect is important to being able to bring civility back into our society.

Now, the Church in the past, needed to be criticized for this type of demonization of certain types of sins, and rightfully so! But lately, it has come from *other* sources. So, let me speak to some of those sources that have created a "closed intellectual" society by "putting down" people of faith!

Professor in a University please listen carefully, if you are <u>so</u> dedicated to open mindedness, then why would you *poke fun* publicly at those who are people of faith? Especially conservative Christians! That is intellectual pride and does not bring admiration to your title as an educator. In your search for knowledge recognize that you are not all-knowing. Pride is not a good tutor in your classroom. A little humility is much more attractive and even winsome. Argue your position, and do it boldly, but "mocking," or "sarcasm" does not become someone of your stature.

To all scientists who highly esteem themselves and their degrees. Please understand that there is a science on the other side (religious based) though you may not agree in some points. Please also understand that there are "other" issues that should be taken into consideration before you build a belief system void of God. Science is important but is not the ultimate answer for understanding the origin of man. It is important that the scientist present "Evolution as a theory," not as factual "science?" Be true to the definitions of what is considered theory and facts, understand the difference. Evolution cannot prove the existence or lack of existence of God. In my humble opinion, evolution is actually more of a leap of faith, than Christianity. For Christianity answers the broad range of questions from suffering, pain, to purpose of life. Can science answer a painful relationship?

Finally, allow me to comment on the media. The other day, I was at a local hospital sitting with a friend while their wife went through some minor surgery. The television in the waiting room was on, and the top two stories of the day were so negative, that no wonder there is skepticism in the world concerning religion. I'm tired of the constant barrage of news, which centers on the moral and ethical failures of religious leaders. Please understand that I am not defending those people. Yet, I hang out with a lot of Pastors, Priests and religious leaders of all faiths. They are for the most part great people. They love their churches and temples, and they are committed to their faith. Why not, every once in a while, do a great story on a church? Why does History channel or Time Magazine articles have to be bent in quoting sometimes "unreliable or obscure" (not even mainstream) sources in order to prove their point? Bring down the rhetoric and share facts and arguments without the stereotypical, rude or even ignorant language that sometimes enters the debate. Media, let's bring civility back to our society.

The third desire that I had for writing this book can be misconstrued. If you thought that this book was about science; or Biblical Criticism (a defense of God's Word), or a rant against Bucknell University or any higher school of education, then you have missed the point of this book. For the point of the Bible, as I stated earlier, is really about God, and His love for you and me!

It's really about a God who loves you and me so much, that He made a way for us to experience forgiveness and salvation, and it is recorded in the Scriptures. Today there is such a disregard for the Bible that I wanted the readers of this book, to understand the following: that God is _real_; that He is _trustworthy_; but mostly, I wanted to share with each reader, that He is _compassionate_. I wanted each reader to know that Christ is the only way! And that he really loves them deeply.

Unfortunately, you can miss the point if you thought this book was only about an evangelical Pastor's weak attempt to prove the improvable. I underscore that this book is more than a defense of the existence of God. It is a revelation of a God who wants to take your life, and make it something special. He wants to forgive your sins, and provide both for your eternal and present life.

Greg Laurie, a Pastor from California tells the story of a man whose name had been mistakenly printed in an obituary column in his local newspaper. Can you imagine waking up in the morning and reading that you are no longer among the living? This man did what any of us would do in the same situation: He went down to the newspaper office and demanded to see the editor. "This is terrible," he told the editor. "Because of your error, I am going to lose a lot of business, because people now think that I am dead!

How could you do that to me?" The editor replied: "I am so sorry for that mistake!" But the man continued to shout at him at the injustice of it all. Finally, the editor had enough, and said, "Alright, buddy. Tomorrow, I'll put your name in the birth column, and you can have a fresh start in life."[62]

Wouldn't it be great if starting over were that easy? Well, that's really the point of the Bible. It is the story of how you and I have sinned against God, as well as others, and how our sins can be forgiven. It is how God puts our lives back together. It is about becoming righteous in God's eyes.

Let me illustrate it with a story from the Bible by a man named Saul of Tarsus. In the New Testament, he experienced one of the most unexpected and radical conversions in the history of the church. It was so unexpected that initially his conversion was greeted by skepticism and suspicion. This man Saul had once dedicated his life to the destruction of the Christian Church. He was a man bent on destroying everything about Christianity. He persecuted men and women who chose to follow Jesus as their Messiah. But he changed, as a result from an encounter that he had with Jesus, on the road to Damascus. This Jewish Zealot who had formally been controlled by hate, was from his conversion controlled by love. A name that would once send chills down the spine of a Christian Saul of Tarsus was transformed into one of the greatest preachers in the history of the Christian Church. In fact, he was even given a new name – *Paul, the Apostle.*

Paul's conversion was such an unlikely event that a British agnostic decided that it would be very easy to disprove it. He set out to prove that the New Testament lacked credibility. He set out to undermine the foundation of the Christian faith by "getting to the truth about this man Paul." The man's name was *George Lyttleton*. He wrote a

---

62 Greg Laurie. *Why Believe?* Word Publishing: Dallas, TX. P 143.

book entitled *"Observations on the Conversion and Apostleship of Saint Paul"* (written in 1747). But his conclusion was remarkably different from his original theses. What did he discover? Paul's conversion and apostleship demonstrated that the Bible was of Divine revelation. [63]

In the midst of trying to prove Christianity false, he ended up meeting the same Jesus who had changed Saul of Tarsus so dramatically on the road of Damascus. He became a believer after studying about the same Jesus who had changed Saul of Tarsus. George Lytteton had thought it was not possible for a man so opposed to the Church, to become a believer. But he found out that it is possible.

The story of how Saul of Tarsus became the Apostle Paul shows that no one is beyond redemption. That's a great lesson for all of us. It shows, that it doesn't matter how radical we once were; it doesn't matter how hard-hearted we may currently be. It doesn't matter what lifestyle we may be trapped in. There is hope for each and all of us.

In fact, there are various lessons we can learn from this man's life. Let me give you five lessons.

Lesson #1: Christianity is not about Religion!

Who was Saul of Tarsus? He was a young man who never did anything half-heartedly. Saul was raised in a strict Jewish home. He learned the scripture as young boy. His family tree sprouted from the best soil. He was of the tribe of Benjamin – the tribe of Israel's first king, Saul. Possibly Saul of Tarsus was even named after him. Saul decided early in his life to go into the ministry. He became a Pharisee, which meant that he was a highly dedicated religious individual, a rather disciplined student of the Scriptures. Because of

---

63 George Lyttleton. *Observations on the Conversion and Apostleship of Saint Paul.* General Books Publication. 1805,2009.

their intense jealousy, the Pharisees were the prime movers behind the crucifixion of Jesus. It just goes to show how religion can be a blinding and destructive force. There have been many horrible crimes and sins committed in the name of religion throughout history; sadly some even in the name of Christianity. I know people who will not listen to a gospel message because of abuses to them in the name of the cross and Jesus. No, Christianity is not about Religion as Saul understood.

Lesson #2: Christianity is not about doing Good Works!

Saul, a religious man, convinced he was doing the right thing. He was a man who was completely committed to HIS religion. But he was actually fighting God. Saul did not persecute the church because he was a bad man. He did it because he thought that he was following religious truth – just doing what was right. He honestly believed that these strange people known as Christians were a menace to God. He thought that the work he was involved in was good and it was even sanctioned by his religion at the time. But following his conversion he wrote, "I did it ignorantly in unbelief" (1 timothy 1:13).

Later, Saul became a member of the Supreme Court of that day – the Jewish <u>Sanhedrin</u> – where he enjoyed fame and influence. He had risen to the top of his profession. This is where we are introduced to him in Acts 8.

> *And Saul was there, giving approval to his death. On that day a great persecution broke out against the church at Jerusalem, and all except the apostles were scattered throughout Judea and Samaria. Godly men buried Stephen and mourned deeply for him. But Saul began to destroy the church.*

> *Going from house to house, he dragged off men*
> *and women and put them in prison. (Acts 8:1-3)*

What motivated Saul? Why was he filled with so much hatred and venom? Acts 7:54-60 records the following reasons. It is a dramatic account of the death of the first martyr of the Christian Church, a courageous young man known as Stephen. Stephen stood before the Sanhedrin and boldly proclaimed his faith in Christ. Acts 7 reads:

> *When they heard this, they were furious and*
> *gnashed their teeth at him. But Stephen, full of*
> *the Holy Spirit, looked up to heaven and saw the*
> *glory of God, and Jesus standing at the right hand*
> *of God. "Look," he said, "I see heaven open and the*
> *Son of Man standing at the right hand of God."*
> (Acts 7:54-56)

Then, in Acts 7:57 and 58, it said…

> *At this they covered their ears and, yelling at*
> *the top of their voices, they all rushed at him,*
> *dragged him out of the city and began to stone*
> *him. Meanwhile, the witnesses laid their clothes*
> *at the feet of a young man named Saul.*

Then, in the most dramatic portion of this death, we read, "*While they were stoning him, Stephen prayed, "Lord Jesus, receive my spirit.*" Then he fell on his knees and cried out, "Lord, do not hold this sin against them." When he had said this, he fell asleep (AC 7:59-60).

What a powerful testimony this was to Saul. Even in the face of death. Stephen was praying for mercy for the ones who were responsible for his death.

It reminds of Jesus hanging on the cross, when he said: "*Father, forgiven them for the do not know what they are doing"* (Luke 23:34). That statement radically transformed the attitude and outlook of one of the thieves crucified beside Jesus who turned to Him in a moment and with a flash of belief said, in Luke 23:42-43: *Then he said, "Jesus, remember me when you come into your kingdom." "Jesus answered him, "I tell you the truth, today you will be with me in paradise."*

As Stephen made a similar plea to the Lord, it apparently penetrated the hardened heart of Saul of Tarsus. Now, initially Stephen's plea caused Saul's heart to grow harder. He began to persecute believers even more zealously. Saul used the occasion of Stephen's trial and execution to launch a full scale persecution of the new church. He carried off converts, both men and women, to prison. He even obtained extradition papers from the High Priest and set off to Damascus 140 miles away from Jerusalem to arrest more Christians. Some believers escaped his net and fled. Therefore, Paul planned to hunt them down and drag them back. No one was going to get away with worshipping Jesus as long as Saul was around!

But an unexplained thing happened on his journey.

> *Meanwhile, Saul was still <u>breathing out murderous threats</u> against the Lord's disciples. He went to the high priest and asked him for letters to the synagogues in Damascus, so that if he found any there who belonged to the Way, whether men or women, he might take them as prisoners to Jerusalem. As he neared Damascus on his journey, suddenly a light from heaven flashed around him. He fell to the ground and heard a voice say to him, "Saul, Saul, why do you persecute me?" "Who are you, Lord?" Saul asked. "I am Jesus, whom you are persecuting," he replied. "Now get up and go into the city, and you will be told what you must do."*

The men traveling with Saul stood there speechless;
they heard the sound but did not see anyone. Saul
got up from the ground, but when he opened his eyes
he could see nothing. So they led him by the hand
into Damascus. For three days he was blind, and
did not eat or drink anything. (Acts 9:1-9)

Up to this point Saul was living on hatred. When it says that he was "*breathing out murderous threats*" it was the same as saying, "the threats were sustaining him." Another translation of the original text states that he was "like a wild beast seeking out his prey." He smelled the blood of Christians. His heart was so filled with hatred and his mind so poisoned with prejudice that he later said that "a raging fury had obsessed him."

Lesson #3 Christianity is about recognizing your own sinfulness.

At that point, however, the resurrected Jesus got a hold of him and the Lord said, *"Why are you persecuting me?"* Imagine how Saul felt at that moment. He asked, *"Who are you Lord?"* He probably was thinking to himself: *"Don't say it's Jesus! Don't say it's Jesus! Don't say it's Jesus!"* And, of course, the Lord replied, *"I AM JESUS."* Saul must have thought: *"Oh, no. I knew He was going to say that. I've been sinning against the very one I thought I was serving."* Imagine how those words must have reverberated through Saul's soul at that moment. He awoke one day to realize that instead of serving God, he had actually been opposing God. For now, he was colliding with Him! What a shock!

Christianity is based on a Biblical principle that <u>men are sinners</u> (Romans 3:23), and <u>cannot</u> saved themselves (Romans 6:23), either by their own good works, or the inability to expunge our own sin through any other source than Christ. Paul, on the road to Damascus, came to that understanding. He realized that "his" good works, or religiosity, could not provide covering for sin.

This is important to realize, because most people have a hard time admitting that they are sinners. That there is no chance of getting to heaven, or having your sins forgiven by some extreme act of religion.

Lesson #4 Christianity is about placing your faith in Christ alone.

At that moment, Saul understood his sin, and committed himself to Jesus Christ. There was an immediate change to Saul's life. Once he recognized who Jesus was, he immediately placed his faith on Him.

- He didn't place his faith on religion.

- He didn't place his faith on good works.

- He didn't place his faith on any other person in history.

- He placed his faith on the Lord Jesus Christ. He understood that his sin was a means of separation from God, and that Christ was the only one who would provide forgiveness.

In Acts chapter 9, and verse 20, we read that Saul, *"At once he began to preach in the synagogues that **Jesus is the Son of God**."*

A little later, Saul was arrested and brought before King Agrippa, a Roman Governor. He re-tells that conversion story on the road to Damascus, and ends with a very clear testimony about the message of the gospel.

> *"So then, King Agrippa, I was not disobedient to the vision from heaven. First to those in Damascus,*

then to those in Jerusalem and in all Judea, and to the Gentiles also, I preached that <u>they should repent and turn to God and prove their repentance by their deeds</u>. That is why the Jews seized me in the temple courts and tried to kill me. But I have had God's help to this very day, and so I stand here and testify to small and great alike. I am saying nothing beyond what the prophets and Moses said would happen--that the <u>Christ would suffer and, as the first to rise from the dead, would proclaim light to his own people and to the Gentiles</u>." (Acts 26:19-23)

His message was two-fold:

1. **<u>Repent</u>** – This word means more than just admitting your sins. It means to "change your mind" about it. Repentance is more than "saying you are sorry." It is confessing that you are a sinner, and that your sin is separating you from God, and that you need a Savior – Jesus Christ.

2. **<u>Believe that Jesus is the Christ, the resurrected Savior</u>** - The resurrection is proof that Jesus was truly the Son of God. This is critical to believing in Christianity. Either Jesus is dead today, or He is alive! All of Christianity's trustworthiness stands on the fact of the resurrection. That means, if your denomination, church or Pastor <u>does not</u> believe in the resurrection of Jesus Christ, then they have left "Historical and true" Christianity. And if that is so, they are not preaching the Gospel of Christ, and you should look elsewhere for your faith.

Lesson #5 Christianity produces changed lives

Saul, who after his conversion to being a Christ follower, got a new name – Paul. He no longer was "trying" to please God." He was trusting in the resurrected Lord to forgive every one of his sins." From that forward, he became focused in spreading the message, that if God, through Christ, could forgive HIS sins, He could certainly forgive all of our (your and mine) sins.

Conclusion

That's the point of this book. It is not to convince you of facts for the sake of apologetics. It is to point you to Jesus Christ. Think about it. *A lot of the stories in New Testament are about people turning from dependence on their own good works to get them to heaven, to a dependence on Jesus Christ.*

God hates sin. But He loves you and me with everlasting love. And he has provided a way for you to feel total forgiveness for every one of your sins, so that if you would die, you would be able to enter into heaven.

But forgiveness of sins is not just about when you die.. It is about the present. In 1930, an unusual event took place. It is still an open case with the FBI missing persons file. On August 15, after dining out with his family, a New York State Supreme Court justice named Joseph Crater hailed a taxi and was never seen or heard from again. The FBI thought the disappearance might be work related, but all investigations ended in a dead end. The only clue was left for his wife and family. It was note that read: "*I am very, very tired. Love Joe.*"[64] That was it. That was the last anyone heard from him.

I think a lot of people today feel that way. Jesus has something to say to the person who is exhausted, and to the

---

64 Wikipedia.org/Joseph Force Crater.

person who is trying hard in life to feel satisfaction, but is hurting. In Matthew 11, we read these words:

> *"Come to me, all you who are weary and burdened, and I will give you rest. Take my yoke upon you and learn from me, for I am gentle and humble in heart, and you will find rest for your souls. For my yoke is easy and my burden is light"* (Matthew 11:28-30).

An expanded translation of this same verse goes like this:

> *"Come here to me all you who are growing weary to point of exhaustion and who have been loaded with burdens and are bending beneath their weight. I alone can cause you to cease from your labor and take away your burdens and refresh you with rest." (LBT)*

That is what Christianity is all about. This is what the Christian walk with Christ is all about. It is about taking people who are tired of running after religion (just like Saul/Paul), and giving them Christ.

How about you?

Is it possible for you to change? Is there really a fresh start available to us through Christ? Yes. Do you want your life to be transformed like Saul's? You can experience these things right now. And you won't need to have your obituary printed in the newspaper in order to have be "born again." All you need is come to Jesus.

But how is that done?

1. First of all, ***you must recognize that you are a sinner***. Realize that you have missed the mark. This is true of each of us. We have deliberately

crossed the line not just once, but many times. if The Bible says: *"For all have sinned and fall short of the glory of God"* (Romans 3:23). This is a hard admission for many to make. It's easier to put the blame for our indiscretions and sins, on bad parenting. But if we are not willing to hear the bad news, we cannot appreciate and respond to the Good News.

2. Second, ***we must realize that Jesus Christ died on the cross for us***. Because of sin, God had to take drastic measures to reach us. Therefore, he came to this earth and walked here as a man. But Jesus was more than just a good man. He was the God/Man – God incarnate- that's why his death on the cross is so significant. For at the Cross, God himself – in the person of Jesus Christ – took our place and bore our sins. He paid for them and purchased our redemption.

3. Third, ***we must repent from or sins***. God has commanded men everywhere to repent. Acts 3:19 states: *"Repent, then, and turn to God, so that your sins may be wiped out, that times of refreshing may come from the Lord."* What does the word "repent" mean? It means to "change direction" – "to hang a U-turn on the road of life". It means to stop living the kind of life we led previously and start living the kind of life outlined in the pages of the Bible. Now we must change and be willing to make a break from the past.

4. Fourth, ***we must receive Jesus Christ into our hearts and lives***. Being a Christian is having God take residence in our lives. John 1:12 tells

us, *"Yet to all who received him (Jesus Christ), to those who believed in his name, he gave the right to become children of God."*

We must receive Him. Jesus said, *"Here I am! I stand at the door and knock. If anyone hears my voice and opens the door, I will come in and eat with him, and he with me"* (Revelation 3:20). Each of us must individually decide to open the door.

Take Notice!

Those of you who think that at the end of your life, God will weigh your good deeds and as long as you have more good than bad, then you will go to heaven…need to read Ephesians 2:8-9 one more time. Also, think of it this way: *IF YOU AND I COULD GET TO HEAVEN ON OUR GOOD WORKS OR DEEDS, THEN WHY DID GOD PUT HIS SON THROUGH SUCH PAIN AND SACRIFICE*! ? That would be a pretty mean Heavenly Father, to put His Son through the pain and agony of death on a cross, if he didn't have to!

How do we open the door of our hearts and receive the gift of eternal life? Through faith and one of the ways is through prayer.

If you never asked Jesus Christ to come into your life, you can do it right now. Here is a sample prayer to help you. God knows your desire to make him the Lord of your life, and this prayer can help you put into words what your desire may be.

> *Lord Jesus I know that I am a sinner and I am sorry for my sin. I turn and repent of my sins right now. Thank you for dying on the cross for me and paying for the price for my sin. Please come into my*

heart and life right now. Fill me with your Holy Spirit, and help me to be your disciple. Thank you for forgiving me, and coming into my life. Thank you that I am now a child of yours, and that I am going to heaven. In Jesus' name, I pray, Amen.

As you pray this prayer, God promises to respond to you. You have made the right decision – the decision which will impact how you spend eternity. If you prayed that prayer, and really meant it, God will welcome you into heaven, but will also provide peace in your life in the present time on earth. This is a decision you will never regret!

If you have questions about your commitment to follow Christ, or want to dialogue further, email us at lewisburgalliance@dejazzd.com

or stop by our church - www.lewisburgalliance.com

A Final Word About
Reasonable Faith

T he goal and theme of this book has been to share that being a person who believes in the Bible is rational. It is reasonable to have a strong believe system in a sovereign God, who loved all of humanity, and who sacrificed himself for the sake of all sinners.

In the beginning of this book, I mentioned Dr. Ben Carson, renown surgeon, whom just by being introduced as a speaker at Bucknell University created a controversy. Allow me the freedom of quoting from his commencement speech. For at the end of the speech (Bucknell University, May 23, 2010), he summarized it well.

> *Do you realize that, in this state, in 1787, during the Constitutional Convention, when the whole thing was about to break apart because the large states and the small states had such divergent opinions — Benjamin Franklin, the elder statesman, stood up there in front of that crowd and he said, 'Gentlemen, stop. Let's get on our knees and let's pray. Let's ask God to give us wisdom.' And they knelt down and*

they prayed. And when they got up, they put together a 17-page document known as the Constitution of the United States, which is the most spectacular governing document anyone has ever put together.

And you know what? People who say things like that; do they realize that our founding document, our Declaration of Independence, talked about certain inalienable rights given to us by our creator a.k.a. God. Do they realize the Pledge of Allegiance to that flag says we are one nation under God? That most courtrooms in the land on the wall it says In God We Trust — every coin in our pocket, every bill in our wallet says In God We Trust. So if it's in our founding documents, it's in our pledge, it's in our courts and it's on our money, but we're not supposed to talk about it — what in the world is that?

In medicine we call it schizophrenia, and doesn't that explain a lot of what's going on in our society today? And we need to make it perfectly plain as you go forth, that it's okay to live by Godly principles of loving your fellow man, caring about your neighbor, developing your God-given talents to their utmost so you become valuable to the people around you — of having values and principles that govern your life. If we do that, not only will we remain a pinnacle nation, but we will truly have one nation under God, indivisible, with liberty and justice for all. Thank you. God bless you.[65]

Thank you, Dr. Carson.

---

65 Bucknell University 2010 Commencement Speech by Dr. B. A. Carson. http://www.bucknell.edu/Dr.BenCarson

Breinigsville, PA USA
05 April 2011
259228BV00001B/14/P